MW01273943

Please accept
the return of
your cheque
Cheers,

Stu

ONE MAN'S WAR

This is the story of a 19 year old Canadian prairie boy, who leaves his small rural community in 1938 and travels to England to join the Royal Navy and become a naval carrier pilot. The clouds of war are already thickening over Europe as he begins his flying training.

As war begins, and with minimum experience, he is thrust into battle flying Skua fighters. First, during the abortive Norwegian campaign flying cover for the embattled, outnumbered, British army from the new British carrier HMS *Ark Royal*, then he is engaged in flying sorties to assist in the evacuation of the army.

Next he is back once more flying off Norway as the Royal Navy attempts to gain revenge for the recent sinking of the British aircraft carrier HMS *Glorious* and her escorts by the German battle cruisers. The Royal Navy then mounts a desperate strike against a powerful German fleet anchored in Trondjeim harbour, which is strongly protected by heavy anti aircraft batteries and the nearby lethal German fighters.

Flying slow and obsolescent dive bombers, the British carrier strike verges on the suicidal. The carrier strike force is virtually destroyed in this doomed attack, and many of the aircrew either were killed or taken prisoner.

From this point on the story tells, in considerable detail, the life of this young Canadian over the next five years, as he undergoes the dangers of existing as a prisoner of war, including his escape attempts, and constant transfers from one prison camp to another because he is marked by the Germans as a troublesome prisoner.

In this major section of the story are his recollections of some of the major escape attempts from German camps and also his personal involvement in the 'Great Escape' organization, and the tragic aftermath of those that managed to break out of the prison camp at Stalag Luft 3. Also described are various escape devices, techniques and radio receiver equipment assembled and used by the prisoners. The tragic deaths of some of his fellow prisons are recounted.

Finally is a detailed description of the brutal, yet heroic, story of the desperate trek of 10,000 allied prisoners as they are forced to walk during one of the worst winters ever experienced in Western Europe. Exposed to desperate conditions and often lacking the most primitive facilities, these unprepared, weak and near-starving men were compelled by their German captors to travel more than 500 kilometres. Facing appalling conditions of captivity and exposure to the elements the captives were constantly herded from one location to another, as their guards attempted to evade the powerful allied armies closing in from the east and west.

With detailed sketches, accompanying photos and paintings, this is a factual and true story of one man's struggle for survival over five years of war!

© Copyright 2005 Stuart E. Soward. All rights reserved.
No part of this publication may be reproduced, stored in a retrieval system, or transmitted, in any form or by any means, electronic, mechanical, photocopying, recording, or otherwise, without the written prior permission of the author.

Published by Neptune Development (1984).

Library and Archives Canada Cataloguing in Publication

Soward, Stuart E., 1924-
        One man's war : sub lieutenant R.E. Bartlett, RN Fleet
Air Arm pilot / Stuart E. Soward.

ISBN 0-9697229-3-1

        1. Bartlett, R. E. (Richard Edward), 1919-. 2. Great Britain. Royal
Navy. Fleet Air Arm—Biography. 3. Air pilots,
Military—Canada—Biography.
4. Air pilots, Military—Great Britain—Biography. 5. World War,
1939-1945—
Personal narratives, Canadian. I. Title.

D811.B269 2005   940.54'8171
C2005-901519-5

Printed in Canada

ONE MAN'S WAR

ONE MAN'S WAR

SUB LIEUTENANT R.E. BARTLETT
RN FLEET AIR ARM PILOT

BY STUART E. SOWARD

CONTENTS

DEDICATION

This book is humbly dedicated to all those allied prisoners of Germany in World War 2, and in particular to those who took part in the desperate forced exodus from the North Compound of Stalag Luft 3 in the deadly winter months of 1945.

ACKNOWLEDGEMENTS

The author wishes to thank Mr. R.E. Bartlett and Mr. A.J. Hill for their remarkable efforts in recreating these wartime incidents and generously providing their own records, which were essential to enable this story to be written. I would also like to thank my wife Sheila who spent so many hours in formatting, compiling and editing this manuscript.

Finally, I would like to express my appreciation to sculptor Pam Taylor for allowing me to use the silhouette of her memorial POW sculpture on the back cover of this book.

PROLOGUE

Richard E. Bartlett, usually called Dick or 'Dickie', was born in the small rural community of Fort Qu'appelle, Saskatchewan on the 21 April, 1919. His father, Christopher Bartlett better known as 'Barty', was born in Kent, England in 1889 and emigrated from England to Canada in 1910. As a young man he spent a lot of his time engaged in rural activities with his gentlemen farmer friends and neighbours including horseback riding. Being well acquainted with English country life and a working knowledge of the operations involved in dairy farming, Barty felt the experience would be of help in his ambition to establish his own dairy farm in Canada. To assist in furthering his employment opportunities his father, who was a solicitor for Pat Burns & Company of Calgary (a large meat packing firm), had given Barty a letter of introduction.

En route the young man was attracted to the Qu'appelle Valley area some 40 miles north-east of Regina. He finally settled at Fort Qu'Appelle on Echo Lake. Here Barty, after a period of sharing a livery business, settled and with a partner commenced to build up a dairy herd in the Qu'appelle valley adjacent to Echo Lake. However, at the outset of war in 1914, the two men responding to the patriotic need to answer the call to arms decided to toss a coin to determine who would enlist and who would remain behind to manage the dairy farm. As luck would have it Barty's partner lost the toss, proceeded overseas and was later killed in the ensuing frightful carnage of trench warfare. Barty subsequently married a local girl, Dora Smales, and they had six children. The oldest was Chris born in 1917, the second was Dick, followed by three younger sisters Joan, Dora and Beth. Tragically Mrs Bartlett died of pneumonia in 1931 about six months after giving birth to her sixth child, a boy named Humphrey, quickly nicknamed 'Hummer' which he is still called. Dick well remembers the steady procession of housekeepers, many who were of indifferent quality, during those early and difficult years following the death of his mother. He was also keenly aware of his father's heavy burden of raising his young family alone while managing and operating his dairy farm.

During the war years and in the thirties, life was not easy for those working in rural Canada, since the depression of the late twenties was international in scope. Being in the dairy farm business the Bartlett family probably suffered less than the drought stricken prairie grain farmers, but even so, Dick Bartlett clearly recalls those difficult years. A particular problem his father encountered was in attempting to assist his neighbours, while at the same time agonizing over the associated difficulty of collecting an appropriate level of payment for his milk sales from his less fortunate friends and community members.

However, there were considerable benefits in the rural life for young boys growing up in the open outdoors with all the seasonal activities of skiing, skating, swimming, hunting and fishing. Being active in such varied pursuits and spending a major part of their young lives in the unique environment of a small prairie community, tended to instill a positive and adventuresome spirit, which in turn developed both initiative and confidence. In addition there was always the ongoing problems experienced in the continuous struggle and long hours involved in attempting to make the farm a success, an objective requiring the participation of all family members. This in itself required patience and a considerable degree of ingenuity and resourcefulness. Such challenges being encountered on a daily basis in a rural environment were not experienced to the same degree by those growing up in an urban society.

By 1936 Chris Bartlett, with his father's financial assistance, had obtained his private pilot's license. Barty, who had always maintained his connections with England in part through a subscription to the Times of London, noted an advertisement providing an opportunity for Canadians to join the Royal Air Force (RAF) for pilot training. Nineteen year old Chris with his basic pilot qualification was eligible, so that year he proceeded to Halifax, boarded one of the many liners plying the England-Canada route, and enlisted in the RAF.

Dick, at 14 years of age, in the meantime, through the assistance of a neighbour who raised silver foxes, was offered the loan of two pregnant female foxes. In return, a deal was worked out wherein Dick would raise the resulting pups, care for the upkeep of them, and at the end of a year keep half the offspring and return the original two vixen and the remaining half of the pups to the owner. This arrangement, although a lot of work for young Bartlett, worked out to the satisfaction of both parties, and at the end of four years of work Dick was the sole owner of approximately 60 foxes.

Dick graduated from high school in 1938 and once again through a Times advertisement, became aware that the Royal Navy was recruiting both pilots and observers to serve in the newly-formed Fleet Air Arm, which now, for the first time since WW1, was under the control of the Royal Navy and being developed as an integral naval branch.

This policy decision was a long time coming, since the RAF had maintained control of all military flying in the United Kingdom since the new service was formed by the Smuts Committee in 1918. The outcome of this arrangement had proved to be most unsatisfactory for the navy, since the RAF provided the aircrew and maintenance personnel for all Royal Navy aircraft. Indeed, the aircrew flying for the navy were officially described as being members of the Fleet Air Arm of the RAF. Additionally, aircraft designed for naval flying were invariably given a low priority with virtually all aircraft being modified for naval use from original RAF specifications. The Admiralty had fought ceaselessly to regain control of its naval aviation branch, but it was not until 1937 that the final decision was made to pass administrative control over the Fleet Air Arm to the Royal Navy. Protracted negotiations then commenced to implement the transfer process, but it was not until May 1939 that the navy finally achieved full control of the Fleet Air Arm.

The advertisement for naval pilots and observers was one early outcome of the transfer process, and Canada, having contributed over 900 pilots to the Royal Naval Air Service during WW1, was seen as a logical and immediate source of recruits for naval aircrew to serve in the newly approved and rapidly expanding Royal Navy Fleet Air Arm.

Dick, with sufficient funds available from his silver fox enterprise, applied for service in the RN after undergoing a medical exam by his local doctor. There was, however, one possible problem. He had contracted rheumatic fever as a child, with a resulting year of absence from school to recover, and was concerned there would be a notation on his medical records which would adversely affect his eligibility for RN service. His doctor, however, felt that any possible lingering effects would not be detected by the RN doctors and carefully deleted any such reference in Dick's medical file.

So in 1938, at the age of 19, Dick Bartlett was provisionally accepted for service in the Royal Navy Fleet Air Arm. He did not have much interest in following in his brother's steps in the RAF and like an amazing number of prairie boys had always expressed a desire to join the navy. With that primary objective in mind, and his additional strong interest in flying, he thought the Royal Navy would fulfill both his objectives. He did have a backup plan to subsequently enlist in the RAF if his naval pilot career did not materialize.

With sufficient funds to pay for his train fare, a 3rd class ocean passage and live frugally for a month in England, Dick left Fort Qu'appelle in late summer of 1938, as the war clouds were ominously gathering over Europe. This trip in itself was an adventure of sorts with the experience of the long journey by train across the endless prairie, then on through Ontario, Quebec and New York for his passage to England. One minor event with a human interest twist took place when Dick, after leaving the train station at New York, began a search for a reasonably priced hotel for the night prior to departing for England the next day. Well aware that

New York taxi drivers were not renowned for their friendliness to strangers, or anybody else for that matter, he waved down a taxi with a degree of some trepidation. Much to his surprise he found that the driver was a recent English immigrant to America. He not only took Dick to a very suitable hotel in keeping with his finances, but after learning that Dick was on his way to join the Royal Navy, the driver not only picked him up the next morning and dropped him off at his ship's pier, but adamantly refused to accept any payment for the fare.

His arrival at Southampton, England, was a remarkable experience. Dick's father had arranged for him to be met upon arrival by a family friend. Much to Dick's surprise and delight, a chauffeur driven limousine rolled up to the gangway and Dick was ceremoniously swept away to a brief period of luxury that one could only dream about. After a delightful drive through the rolling English countryside to Winchester, the car turned in at the gates of an imposing country estate, passing extensive fields and dairy herds complete with large well-maintained barns and outbuildings. The car finally stopped in front of a magnificent country mansion, with numerous maid servants and what appeared to be a variety of butlers and other men servants. For a young 19 year old Canadian man coming from a small prairie community, to be welcomed and accommodated by virtual strangers in such sumptuous surroundings for a week was truly an experience never to be forgotten.

It was over all too quickly and young Dick Bartlett departed to begin the next phase of his life as a 'colonial' Midshipman in the Royal Navy.

1

ROYAL NAVY PILOT TRAINING

Following his initial acceptance as a Midshipman, with a seven year commission in the Royal Navy, Dick Bartlett went through the usual induction procedure, which also included being outfitted by purchasing his uniforms and kit accessories from Gieves Limited, London. They were probably the oldest suppliers of Royal Navy officers uniforms, having provided uniforms to such a notable officer as Lt. Bligh in 1789, and no doubt to many of his predecessors. The company had a unique and unusually close relationship with the Royal Navy, insofar as the repayment cost of the individual officers' uniform kit was spread over a long period of time, with arrangements made for the payments to be deducted monthly directly from the individual's pay. This ensured that Gieves would always receive payment in full providing the individual officer survived the payout period. In order to counter this eventuality, the company prudently arranged additional security for the debts with an unusual insurance policy, which guaranteed payment of the amount owing should the officer concerned become a fatality before the debt was paid. In the case of the most junior officer in the service, a Midshipman, grossing the princely pay of 5 shillings per day, it would obviously take several years before the debt was repaid.

In November 1938, Midshipman Bartlett proceeded to HMS *Hermes* for his initial six week training. It consisted of an introduction to all the skills held dear by the surface officer, including seamanship, gunnery and watch keeping. This group (Course #3) of young officers consisted of 30 pilot candidates and 30 observer candidates. Those under 21 years of age were assigned the rank of Midshipman and those over 21 years were granted the next higher rank of Sub. Lieutenant. Dick was pleasantly surprised to meet two other Canadians on the pilot training course, Frank Harley and Oswald 'Tats' Tattersall. All three survived the war.

Dick was soon well aware of the obvious class bias that prevailed among the group. The Canadians and Australians were ranked as colonials and this, in the minds of some of the English Public School members, automatically relegated them to a lower rung on the social ladder. Accordingly, the lone Australian and the three Canadians teamed up for their mutual morale and security. They were subsequently labelled the 'Bolshy Colonials'.

As the young Midshipmen began their preliminary naval training they received a somewhat unnerving experience. This consisted of the decidedly unfriendly introductory greeting from the Captain of *Hermes*. His 'welcome speech' began by describing the entire aviator group as "nothing but a rabble, that would continue to be a rabble ". This disquieting and negative attitude was fairly typical of the view held by many senior Royal Navy officers. It was directed primarily at the young men who, as aspiring aviators, were representative of the acknowledged increasing importance of the aircraft carrier. There was a significant cadre in the Royal Navy who suffered from the 'supremacy of the battleship' mentality, and thus considered those who preached or welcomed the considerable benefits of the aircraft and aircraft carrier were both disruptive and misguided.

The Royal Navy in 1938 had six aircraft carriers, consisting of *Argus, Courageous, Eagle, Furious, Glorious* and *Ark Royal.* The first five had all been built in 1924 on cruiser hulls and although capable of high speed, suffered from the fact that their design was now outmoded, generally obsolete and suffered severe limitations in the number and types of aircraft that could be operated. However, an interesting and rather innovative design feature of *Argus* was that the island bridge or control centre was retractable, allowing the structure to be lowered to deck height when operating aircraft. The newly-commissioned *Ark Royal,* on the other hand, was the first of a new generation of armoured deck carriers, having been planned, designed and fitted as a modern carrier. With the exception of *Furious,* all the foregoing carriers were sunk during WW2.

Following the six week introductory familiarization to the Royal Navy, the next six weeks was spent aboard another carrier, in this case *Courageous.* Here the aspiring pilot and observer groups went their separate ways with the thirty pilots continuing aboard with further indoctrination in naval subjects and junior officer training.

Frank Harley clearly recalls as a spectator the first deck landing trials of the new Skua fighter/dive bomber aboard *Courageous*. It was hardly an impressive display! The first aircraft aboard blew a tire on landing and narrowly avoided going over the carrier's side. The second, on landing practically stood on its nose. The third landing was spectacular! The aircraft managed to catch the last wire, but careened into the island superstructure, lost its propeller and reduction gear, then cartwheeled across the deck and flopped over the side into the sea. This terminated the trials.

On completion of the training aboard the carrier, the group proceeded to the Naval College at Greenwich where they boarded during their air training in March 1939 at No. 20 E.R.& F.T.S. an elementary flying training school at Gravesend outside London. Here the students were introduced to their first aircraft, the long-serving Tiger Moth, the sturdy little biplane which was the standard elementary trainer in the RAF. Flying from the grass field they each amassed a grand total of about 50-60 hours of dual instruction and solo flying, successfully realizing their flying ambitions. Ground school instruction was a major part of the syllabus involving aviation subjects such as Theory of Flight, Navigation, and Airmanship.

On a social note, while boarding at the Naval College, Dick Bartlett recalls the genuine friendliness and interest most of the elderly Admirals at the college extended to the young Midshipmen, proffering drinks, which was in marked contrast to the hostile reception shown by the captain on their arrival aboard *Hermes*. Attrition, however, was taking its toll and by the time the students had completed their elementary flying course, two or three had failed to qualify, discontinued training and were offered the opportunity to transfer to observer training.

The next phase of the air training program continued in May at the advanced No. 1 Flying Training School and was conducted at RAF Station Netheravon, which was well known historically to house the oldest RAF Officers Mess in England. The aircraft flown here was the US-built North American Harvard, just recently purchased by the RAF and probably the best advanced trainer available at the time. However, it was an unforgiving aircraft for the unwary or slow to learn. Official records established that four of the young trainees of the 29 students on the course were killed during the six months of advanced flying training, with an additional student killed in a car accident. Dick remembers two of the fatal accidents, the first involved an instructor and a student who were unable to recover from a practice spin, the second occurred when two students were killed while carrying out formation flying. The number of fatalities on the course was unusually high, and in Dick's opinion was partly attributable to lack of experience the RAF instructors had while flying the new Harvards, which were without doubt greatly advanced over the previously flown slower biplanes. As a result, when conducting practice spins, a pilot was much more likely to get into trouble.

The flying hours flown by each student on the Harvard averaged about 100 hours total, with 60-70 hours spent on solo flying. The syllabus was primarily orientated for fighter pilot training, with emphasis on formation flying and basic fighter tactics. It was also at Netheravon, in May, that an Admiralty spokesman first openly raised the prospect of war and bluntly told the young pilots that it was becoming clear that the country would probably be at war by September.

While in training at Netheravon, there was a brief opportunity for Dick to meet with his older brother Chris, now an experienced RAF pilot. Chris had flown to England from the Middle East in a Vickers Valencia bomber for a few days, during which he was exchanging the aircraft for a newer bomber, the Vickers Bombay. Unfortunately time was so short that the two could not get together and Chris flew back to his base in Africa. The two never would meet!

In October 1939, the young naval pilots completed their Service School flying and earned their coveted Royal Navy Fleet Air Arm wings. As ominously forecast, in September, England, France and the British Commonwealth were officially at war and what came to be known as 'the phoney war' phase began.

The next stage of Dick's flying as a naval aviator was in November 1939, when he joined the Torpedo Training Unit at the RN Air Station Gosport. Here he was checked out and flew the Fairey Aviation-built Swordfish. This was a biplane designed from a 1933 RAF specification, calling for an aircraft to carry out the multi roles of torpedo dropping, gunnery spotting and reconnaissance. Saddled with such a variety of roles, and with a maximum speed of less than 120 knots, the aircraft was particularly vulnerable to enemy attack in each role. Interestingly though, and in spite of an excessively high engine failure rate, the Swordfish was one of the few aircraft to remain in service throughout the war.

One reason for its durability was the fact that with such a slow speed it was very difficult for the high speed German fighters to shoot down, and often an experienced

Swordfish pilot could evade the oncoming fighters by flying in small circles at wave top level, which was invariably a difficult target to hit. On the other hand, as events would confirm, the aircraft was a sitting duck when attempting a torpedo attack against heavily defended naval forces.

This six week course consisted of a lot of flying over the sea, camera runs on various targets, formation flying and practice torpedo dropping. One of the more interesting aspects of his indoctrination was catapult launching from the airfield. A particular intriguing procedure when catapulting the Swordfish, was to manually lock the control column with a large lever mounted over the pilot's head. When the launch was activated by the cordite charge in the system, the aircraft was literally shot into the air and when the pilot had regained his composure, he would then unlock the controls and fly away. Total flying on the course was about 20 hours with most flights averaging less than an hour.

Following the Swordfish conversion, Dick Bartlett proceeded to the RN Air Station Donibristle in January 1940, for a two month period flying the Swordfish while attached to 776 Squadron for advanced operational flying. Here the course involved practicing Aerodrome Dummy Deck Landings (ADDLS), instrument flying, formation flying, navigation, practice bombing and rear camera gun practice. Over the two month period Dick flew approximately 16 hours, most of which were of a 30 minute duration, with the majority of flights being concentrating on ADDLS.

Finally ready for his carrier indoctrination, in February Dick proceeded to the French naval base at Toulon, France. The Swordfish pilots were based at Hy'eres, the nearby airfield used during the forthcoming deck landing period aboard the carrier HMS *Argus*. One aspect of the detachment to Toulon was the opportunity to have a night in 'Gay Paree'. One night in Paris was about all a Midshipman could afford, but it was an experience that was worth every shilling.

While at the Hy'eres airfield, it was rather a unique experience to be exposed to the French Navy routine. During flying hours the French operated an open wine bar, which remained active until flying ceased, at which point it was shut down and they all went home. Drinking during flying hours was no doubt merely an expression of a civilized French custom, but it was an unexpected intriguing opportunity for the young Midshipmen. From 11-16 February Dick carried out his deck landing training, successfully completing 14 deck landings and qualified as a carrier pilot with an above average assessment. By this time he had a grand total of over 200 hours flying.

In March 1940 Dick proceeded to the RAF Station at Aldergrove for a two month tour of duty as a staff pilot for the training of naval air gunners. This was not very sophisticated training, since it consisted of either having his back seat gunner firing a somewhat antiquated Lewis machine gun at an air towed drogue target or else in turn towing the drogue and having another aircraft firing at the target. Since the Swordfish aircraft speeds were invariably about 100-110 knots and the range of the Lewis gun was so short, Dick remembers the trainee gunners repeatedly requesting he fly closer to the target because of the difficulty they were experiencing in ascertaining if the tracer bullets were even hitting the drogue.

The aircraft flown during this period were primarily

the Swordfish and the Blackburn Shark with a few sorties flown using the newer Blackburn Roc. The Roc, planned to replace the Skua, was a two seat fighter monoplane with a four gun revolving turret manned by the gunner. This aircraft was developed as a naval equivalent to the RAF Boulton Paul Defiant. The aircraft achieved a mercifully short-lived degree of success against German fighters when first sent into combat at Dunkirk. However, once the German fighter pilots realized the Defiant was a sitting duck by an attack from almost any angle except the rear, it suffered severe losses and was withdrawn quickly from front line service. If nothing else, it was much faster than the Swordfish and Shark, having a maximum speed of 196 mph. Dick's total flying achieved at this flying unit was about 95 hours.

The Skua had begun equipping FAA fighter squadrons in 1938, and was been heralded with great publicity as the most modern aircraft addition to the Royal Navy. While staff flying at Aldergrove, Dick, anxious to fly a more modern aircraft, managed to check out on a newly arrived Skua and flew one air firing sortie. The aircraft was a two seater monoplane intended for a multi naval role, namely as a dive bomber, a fighter and for spotting/recce duties. It was fitted with four forward firing machine guns and a rear firing machine gun operated by the Telegraphist/Air gunner, (TAG). Saddled with such a variety of differing roles, the aircraft suffered accordingly from a variety of limitations.

With a top speed of 225 mph it was too slow to be effective in the fighter role. Also, during initial tests in the dive bombing role, it was found that when flying at a steep angle dive, upon releasing the bomb it promptly dropped into the propellor. A crutch to hold the bomb away from the propellor upon release was therefore installed. An additional modification was also incorporated through relocating the engine forward by about 18 inches. This was accomplished by extending the engine mount with additional tubular framing. Although this helped solve the 'bomb in propellor problem', the flexibility of the engine mounting was also increased. Dick recalls this was graphically apparent when the squadron Senior Pilot, being checked out on the Skua, made a heavy landing on completing his first flight and the engine fell off!

One additional and most disconcerting problem was that often the pilot could not recover the aircraft from a spin. This was hopefully resolved by installing a large parachute in the tail, which would be opened by the pilot when the aircraft got into a spin. The theory behind this concept was that the chute would stop the spinning mode, and the pilot would then jettison the chute. In actual practice, the first phase of the concept was successful insofar as the spinning did stop. But unfortunately the aircraft dropped like a stone after the chute release, and invariably ended up making a large hole in the ground or a big splash in the sea.

Operationally, the Skuas, when first in squadron use, encountered the usual teething problems. In late September 1939, two Skuas flown by Lt. Thurston, RN and Royal Marine Capt. Griffon, carried out a bombing attack on a German U Boat. As luck would have it, their bomb firing mechanism was not properly adjusted with a time delay. Both aircraft were so badly damaged by their own bomb explosions that they crashed practically alongside the submarine. They were forced to accept the invitation of the submarine's captain to come aboard with him, subsequently becoming two of the first British naval prisoners of war. (POWs.)

Another undesirable feature of the Skua was that, unlike new aircraft being built in the United States, the fuel tank was not self-sealing. To overcome this deficiency the British Admiralty resorted to a rather quaint solution. Each Skua crew was issued, and signed as having received, a small bag containing a number of different sized corks. In the event of the aircraft's fuel tank being perforated by enemy action, the plan was for the rear gunner to examine the hole(s), select an appropriate-sized cork and manually plug this into the leak. This solution was naturally the subject of considerable amusement and scepticism by the Skua crews. One could hardly imagine during an aerial battle, that the gunner would stop firing his machine gun, stretch out into the slipstream (assuming the fuel tank was not on fire) and attempt to reach and plug a fuel leak with hopefully a cork of the correct size. To add insult to injury, the crews were responsible to account periodically for any deficiency in the number of corks issued.

The Skua, in spite of its shortcomings, was flown with both courage and skill by the FAA pilots, as the British carriers *Ark Royal* and *Glorious* were deployed to cover the British army landings in the Trondjeim area of Norway. Although suffering losses, the Skuas in their role of fighters had considerable success against the German bombers. In addition, 800 and 803 FAA Squadrons, flying Skuas from Hatson in the Orkneys, achieved a remarkable victory on 10 April, 1940, when flying at their extreme range, dive bombed the German light cruiser *Konigsberg* at Bergen, Norway. The already damaged cruiser was hit by a number of 500 lb. bombs dropped by the force of 16 Skuas and went to the bottom. Only one Skua failed to return.

It was in late April 1940, during this staff flying

period, that Dick's squadron was contacted by the Admiralty one night to determine if there were any replacement Skua pilots available to join the carrier squadrons currently assigned for the Norwegian Campaign. Dick Bartlett, now promoted to Sub. Lieutenant, effective his 21st birthday in March, and Sub. Lieutenant G.P. Williams, had each flown the Skua. Unbeknownst to them, the RAF squadron adjutant kindly volunteered their names. Both were immediately accepted and promptly re-assigned to 759 squadron at RN Air Station Eastleigh for a brief fighter course. Here Dick flew three different aircraft, all of which were obsolescent, but with no other suitable aircraft available were still classed in the general category of a naval fighter. Over the next three weeks Dick flew about 15 hours, primarily in the Skua and the Gladiator. The latter, although a biplane, was the fastest at 357 mph, a delight to fly, and fitted with four forward firing guns. The Gladiator was still considered to be operationally effective and later, during the desperate days of the Battle of Britain, did serve briefly in a few RAF fighter squadrons. Dick also flew a formation and a target sortie in the Roc. His flying while on this short fighter course concentrated on formation, dive-bombing and dummy deck landings preparatory to joining a Skua operational carrier squadron.

On 31 May, 1940, he completed his operational training, was now a qualified fighter pilot, and with a grand total of less than 9 hours of Skua flying time, Dick Bartlett was appointed to 803 Fighter Squadron currently serving aboard HMS *Ark Royal.*

RN Aviation Midshipmen aboard HMS Courageous 1938. Left, Canadian O.W. Tattersall, Right. Canadian R.E. Bartlett, Center, D.P. Wellings, killed during WW2.

Swordfish aircraft deck landing. Credit Imperial War Museum A8336.

Gloster Gladiator. Last RAF biplane fighter used in WW2.

Sub Lt. Dick Bartlett with Gladiator.

Blackburn Roc entered RN service 1939. Roc was naval version of RAF Defiant.

Blackburn Skua fighter/dive bomber. Entered RN service in 1938.

2

-AT WAR-
THE FAA NORWEGIAN
CAMPAIGN

On 31 May, 1940, S/Lt. Dick Bartlett, with his Telegraphist/Air gunner N/A Lloyd Richards, flew their Skua from RNAS Hatson in the Orkneys to join 803 Squadron aboard HMS *Ark Royal,* the Royal Navy's newest carrier. The other squadron appointed to the carrier was 800 Squadron, also equipped with Skuas. In addition, there were two squadrons of Swordfish aboard. *Ark Royal* proceeded to a position off the coast of Norway, where the dual role of the two squadrons was to fly fighter patrols over the fleet and support the British army engaged in battle against the German land forces in Norway.

The fighter patrols over the fleet were fairly straight forward and routine, but the army support role was a very different and difficult role. The first problem was that the only maps available to the pilots were Admiralty coastal charts, which provided little topographical information other than the location of the coastal mountains. Navigation was therefore tricky, since the individual pilot had to locate a specific mountain for a departure point in order to accurately fly out to intercept the carrier's estimated position. This new position was based on a projected position of the carrier some four hours different from takeoff position of the aircraft. Since radio silence was strictly enforced and navigational accuracy of the pilot was at times unavoidably inaccurate, it was not unusual for an aircraft to break out of cloud and fail to sight the fleet or, if the pilot did locate the fleet, there was always the ongoing risk of being greeted with a burst of gunfire from the protective screen of destroyers escorting the larger ships. On occasion, since the only communication for identification purposes was by the aircraft firing a Very flare, the invariable response from the destroyers was a blast of anti-aircraft fire, since the ships believed they were under attack. The Skua pilots being on the receiving end, optimistically held to the hope that if the level of accuracy of the destroyers' gunnery was on a par with that of their aircraft recognition, there was little to fear.

An interesting departure from the normal carrier landing procedure was in operation aboard *Ark Royal.* Instead of the normal practice of lowering then raising the barriers on the flight deck after each arrested landing, followed by the aircraft taxiing forward to the deck park area, the barriers of the *Ark Royal* were retained in the lowered position. In this process, as each aircraft landed aboard with the barriers down, if the aircraft missed the wires the pilot merely proceeded to take off again. In a normal landing with a wire engaged, the aircraft was taxied forward after disengaging the wire and then immediately lowered down the forward lift to the hangar deck below. This rather unusual procedure, with no barriers in operation, certainly eliminated any aircraft running into a barrier. On the other hand it greatly extended the time the carrier was vulnerable to submarine or air attack due to the long landing interval while steering into wind and the extra time it took for each aircraft to be lowered to the hangar deck. With regard to the Skua, Dick Bartlett remembers that on one occasion he inadvertently forgot to lower his hook. Rather than flying away, he actually managed to stop his Skua by the skilful application of brakes without nosing it over as he came to a stop abreast the island superstructure.

Initially, upon joining the Fleet Air Arm, but particularly during these early operations, Dick experienced a degree of cultural shock regarding his English fellow pilots. He was surprised that many of them were long-haired, used cologne and were dressed wearing a handkerchief hanging out of their sleeve. As a result he wondered what kind of an organization he had joined. However, after a somewhat dangerous mission, they would often describe it as, "Wasn't that fun! Lets go for a drink." As Dick was to relate, he being less sanguine in nature seriously wondered on such occasions whether he had better first check his underwear before heading to the bar.

It should be remembered that these few FAA squadrons, with their young and inexperienced pilots, flying obsolete and obsolescent aircraft, under questionable senior leadership, against a well-equipped professional enemy, were the initial core of the new naval Fleet Air Arm. Those who survived the first two years of operations continued to display their exuberance, lack of reverence and carefree spirit. While doing so they developed a remarkable esprit de corps as their experience and flying skills improved under combat, often against heavy odds. They subsequently established the *modus operandi* and leadership standards for their young and rapidly expanding Fleet Air Arm Branch.

With the unfolding disaster taking place in the overrunning of France and the Lowlands, the evacuation of the British army in Norway was a foregone conclusion, and in early June 1940 the outnumbered British forces commenced the withdrawal of the army from Narvik. During this period the Skuas of *Ark Royal* were carrying out bombing attacks and fighter patrols in general support.

At this time of year during the Norwegian campaign, there was virtually continuous daylight with 24 hours of flying in effect. The British fleet was now operating about 150 miles off the coast of Narvik and the Skuas would take off in flights of three, carrying a 500 lb. bomb with their four forward machine guns fully armed, and the air gunner manning his old Lewis gun. Dick described the Skua like flying a bathtub. It was sadly underpowered, but its best feature was that it went 'downhill' very fast. The aircraft could take quite a bit of flak damage and in practice, if an aircraft returned without flak damage, the captain of the carrier assumed the pilot had not pressed home the attack. Dick found that coming back with flak damage to his aircraft was easily accomplished since the German anti aircraft defences were both accurate and heavy.

Flying around the clock was intensive and the aircrews became exhausted very quickly. Operations consisted of maintaining two fighter patrols over the evacuation area and two more aircraft over the transfer point, where the small boats loaded with troops would be loaded on to the larger transports. Each patrol lasted two hours and regardless of whether any of the pilots had expended all their ammunition in the first ten minutes, the aircraft would remain on task until relieved. As Dick later recounted, the Skuas were fortunate in one sense due to the nearby presence of RAF Hurricanes still based at Narvik. As a result, when the Skuas attacked the German bombers, the crews often believed the Skuas were Hurricanes and split up and broke off their attacks on the evacuation area, not realizing the Skuas were not only out of ammunition but also not Hurricanes. Nevertheless it was very hazardous flying unarmed over the combat zone, facing both German fighters and bombers while pretending to be an armed and dangerous Skua fighter pilot.

After the army evacuation the aircraft carrier HMS *Glorious,* in a highly questionable Admiralty decision which was covered up for many years, departed from the main fleet with only two destroyers as escort and proceeded independently to the UK. En route, with not even any protective or scouting aircraft in the air, the small force was intercepted by the German battle cruisers *Scharnhorst* and *Gneisenhau.* In the ensuing chase the three British ships were attacked and sunk with a great and tragic loss of life totalling 1519 personnel, including virtually all the RAF squadron. The aircraft aboard were all lost with the carrier, including the RAF squadron's precious Hurricanes which had been evacuated from their Norwegian airfield and flown aboard *Glorious* with great skill by their pilots.

After decades of silence, since broken by diligent research, it was established that the prime reason for *Glorious* to return independently to England was to enable the captain of the carrier, a submariner with no aviation experience, to initiate a court martial against the commander of the carrier's Air Department. Apparently the commander, an experienced airman, had expressed serious misgivings about what he considered the captain's questionable and overriding decisions concerning the general employment of the carrier's aircraft. It was the air commander's view that such decisions would invariably result in serious aircraft and crew losses with little or nothing to be gained. The captain died when the carrier went down!

HMS Ark Royal 1940. First of new armoured deck carriers at anchor.

HMS Ark Royal launching and recovering Swordfish 1940.

HMS Glorious aircraft carrier 1939.

Blackburn Swordfish from Dick Bartlett's collection. Painting by Colin Pattle.

Range of Skua fighters ready for launching. HMS Ark Royal 1940.

3

SKUA STRIKE ON SCHARNHORST

Following the return of *Ark Royal* to the UK, the carrier was almost immediately assigned back to the Norwegian area to recommence further operations against German naval forces. On the morning of 12 June, improving weather allowed air operations to begin and three Skuas were launched for defensive patrols over the fleet as the ships headed eastward.

By Thursday 13 June, 1940, *Ark Royal* was approximately 200 nautical miles north-west of Trondjeim harbour in Norway. This was the launching position for a planned dive bombing strike of 15 Skuas, timed for shortly after midnight from *Ark Royal*, against German naval units based at Trondjeim. This naval force was believed to include the battle cruiser *Scharnhorst*, a Hipper Class cruiser, and other smaller cruisers and destroyers.

The proposed attack by the Skuas was timed to strike the German ships at 0200, 13 June. Simultaneously, an RAF diversionary attack was scheduled by four 18 Group Beaufort bombers on Vaernes, the Luftwaffe fighter base adjacent to Trondjeim. As part of the overall British strike force, was the addition of six twin-engine Blenheim Mk. IV fighter bombers of 18 Group, which were to rendezvous with the *Ark Royal* in the role of a fighter escort for the departing Skua dive bombers. A group of Swordfish aircraft from the carrier were also assigned to carry out a torpedo attack on the anchored ships. Fortunately, and no doubt to the immense relief of the Swordfish pilots involved, this plan was discarded. This would have been suicidal with the 110 knot Swordfish flying along the narrow fjord in broad daylight heading directly at the heavily armed naval ships, while simultaneously under attack by German fighters.

Dick recalls that there was considerable concern expressed by the two Skua squadron commanders, Lt. Cdr. J Casson and Royal Marine Capt. R.T. Partridge, about the tactical aspects and overall chances of a successful mission. First, the under-powered Skuas, each loaded with a 500 lb. bomb, with only minimal fighter escort, would be slow and vulnerable to attack by the German Me 109 and 110 fighters known to be based nearby. The landfall for the strike was the island of Froya off the Norwegian mainland. From this position, the Skua attackers would, of necessity, be crossing the coast in plain view and flying eastward in formation for about 60 miles (about 30 minutes flying time) along the fjord leading to the targets in the harbour. In such a situation they would be unable to take any significant avoiding action because of the necessity to position themselves accurately to dive into the heavily defended anchorages of the German warships, which were additionally protected by the surrounding mountainous terrain.

Capt. Partridge, for one, was well aware of the powerful air defences the Germans had established around the Trondjeim area. During the recent strikes the Royal Navy had mounted against the Germans, Partridge had been engaged in aerial battles with the Luftwaffe and in one instance had achieved a degree of success. While flying his Skua he successfully shot down a Dornier bomber in one engagement and in following it down saw it crash land at the end of a frozen lake in a great cloud of snow.

The sequel to this success was quite unusual! Partridge's aircraft engine suddenly quit but he successfully force landed on the same lake. It was late afternoon by this time so he and his crewman found a cabin on the shoreline, and in no time were quite warm and comfortable in front of a blazing fire. About 2 a.m., much to their surprise the German Dornier crew walked in, each armed with revolvers. From this moment on the two groups uneasily and warily ignored each other, occupying opposite ends of the small cabin until dawn. At this point Partridge and his crewman decided it would be prudent to make their departure. They had not gone very far before they were intercepted by a Norwegian ski patrol, who, assuming they were German, were quite prepared to shoot them right then and there. Fortunately Partridge had time to produce a half crown with the king's head on it and persuaded the patrol that they were indeed British allies. The entire group then proceeded back to the cabin, but upon them opening the door one of the German crew instinctively reached for his revolver and was promptly shot by the Norwegians. The remainder of the German crew were the next candidates for execution, but

Partridge persuaded the Norwegians instead to take them as prisoners of war. After the war, in an interesting turn of events, Partridge tracked down the captain of the Dornier crew and they subsequently became good friends.

Aboard the carrier, and providing support for the collective serious misgivings of the airmen, it was understood the captain of *Ark Royal* had sent a message to the Admiralty expressing his doubts about the viability of the planned mission. The Admiralty was adamant, however, and the operation was ordered to proceed.

There was a general feeling in the squadrons that this planned attack was largely an attempt to retaliate for the recent needless loss of the carrier *Glorious* and her two escorts. It was becoming obvious to those involved in the attack that it was a highly dangerous mission, bordering on the suicidal, which at best could only be marginally justified. Further, the diversionary and simultaneous attack by the RAF bombers was of key importance. Additionally important was the provision of the Blenheim fighter escort to achieve a degree of diversionary protection, hopefully enabling the Skuas to carry out a successful dive bombing attack during the expected air battle between the Blenheims and the German Me.109 and Me.110 fighters.

However, it is important to review the RAF aircraft situation in 18 Group in early 1940. Pilot Officer Joe Hill of 254 Squadron, recalls the brief history of the squadron commencing in January 1940, when the unit was transferred to Coastal Command and shortly after began equipping with the Mk. IVF Blenheim (Fighter) aircraft. This aircraft was the long-nosed version, and was fitted with a Browning .303 machine gun (mg.) in the port wing and a Vickers .303 (mg.)

in a turret for rearward air defence. Four Browning (mgs.) facing forward were mounted in a pod under the fuselage, which was primarily the justification for classing the Mk. IV in the fighter category. Additional fuel tanks outboard of each engine were fitted, to provide more fuel for the intended area of operations, namely the North Sea and Norwegian coast. This extra fuel extended the endurance to a total of 6½ to 6¾ hours. Overall, however, the increases in armament and fuel made the Mk. 1VF slower by 10-15 mph than the bomber version of the Blenheim. The economical cruising speed of the aircraft was about 170 mph or 145 knots.

In April the squadron went into action and Joe Hill flew several sorties over the German-held Norwegian coast. By May several of the crews had failed to return and "A" flight in particular suffered the loss of two Flight Commanders in only two days. One of the squadron's roles was to attempt to locate the *Scharnhorst*, which was believed hiding in Trondjeim Fjord. On 9 June, in a mission to Trondjeim, Joe Hill, flying with clear weather en route but with the welcome benefit of cloud cover over Norway, was able to pop out of cloud, sight two heavy warships and disappear back into cloud as anti-aircraft guns opened up. The sightings confirmed the location of the heavy German naval units, and for the next few days sorties were continued by the Blenheims to ensure the ships were still there.

Just days later the Admiralty came forward with the request for Blenheim fighter escort to rendezvous with the *Ark Royal* and accompany the Skuas in a joint strike against the *Scharnhorst*. As a result of the previous heavy losses in aircraft and aircrew, the Blenheim squadron was only able to provide five aircraft, and Joe Hill, as a member of "B" flight and having had the most Norwegian operational experience, was designated as the second flight leader. This was a hazardous operation for the Blenheims, since the overall duration of the mission left only enough fuel for a few minutes combat flying over the target area, with a marginal amount remaining for the return flight.

Aboard the *Ark Royal*, on the afternoon before the mission, following the initial briefing, most of the aircrew tidied up their cabins and wrote letters home to be posted in the event they did not make it back to the carrier. Dick decided that it would be better if he did not write home, preferring his father to think his son had died quickly and unexpectedly, rather than receiving any written hints suggesting the futility of the planned strike. The gloom at the night briefing was evident and as expected it was both brief and grim. The tactical aircraft plan was to deploy the two squadrons with the first (803) to dive bomb the *Scharnhorst* in a direction from bow to stern and 800 squadron to simultaneously attack from the reverse direction. Finally, in view of the circumstances, the bar was opened enabling the pilots a final opportunity to partake of a 'double' prior to the midnight launch.

Dick Bartlett recalls that the Skuas were all free deck launched and cannot recall whether the aircraft were actually fitted and had the capability for a catapult launch. In any event, because the 15 aircraft took virtually all the available deck space, there was no room left to fly off a larger strike force. The takeoffs, although requiring a longer run, were uneventful, but the time to form up and get into formation was excessive for the slow-climbing Skuas as they climbed to 11,000 feet, burdened with full fuel, ammunition and carrying a 500lb. armour-piercing bomb. Dick remembers with a bit of humour that his three plane flight leader, Lt. D.C. Gibson (later Vice Admiral Sir Donald Gibson), had initially and inadvertently left his flaps in the take off position, which slowed the aircraft and delayed the forming up on the strike leader's flight.

Dick also clearly recalls the beautiful clear blue sky as the strike formation climbed away in the 'midnight sun'. He also seriously wondered if it would be the last sunrise he would ever witness. The overall flying time en route to the Norwegian coast was about two hours.

The first sign of trouble became apparent when the RAF Blenheim fighter escort failed to appear and rendezvous with the Skuas as they departed over *Ark Royal.* The carrier strike were now forced to proceed on their own with no protective cover.

On schedule, about 0130 a.m., the Skua strike force reached their landfall at Froya Island and headed into the fjord opening into Trondjeim Fjord which led to the harbour. In addition to a number of lighthouses in the entrance and unknown to the British, there was also a German lookout established at the entrance. The attacking force was instantly reported and tracked as it flew along the fjord.

From this point on the attack was in considerable jeopardy. The first major problem was created by the RAF force of Beauforts. Unfortunately they had arrived earlier than the planned 2 a.m. attack on their airfield target. This of course resulted in the German fighters being alerted, airborne and already in action.

During the 60 mile run along the fjord, Dick clearly recalls the last few miles with a deep sense of foreboding, but also noted the beauty of the rising sun and the electric blue of cloudless sky, as they followed the fjord in a northeast easterly heading. He also wryly commented much later that it would probably have been less hazardous if there had been some protective cloud cover. Then ahead, he could see the German ships anchored in the harbour just north of the city of Trondjeim.

Next, the intense and accurate anti aircraft fire from the ships and shore batteries enveloped the two leading flights as they prepared to dive onto their targets. Simultaneously, the Me.109 and Me.110 enemy fighters commenced their attacks, relentlessly zeroing in on the vulnerable Skuas in swift attacks from behind and on the beam swarming around the slowly approaching British aircraft. Already the lead aircraft were under fire and Dick could see Skuas going down in smoke and flames. From this point on, during the confusion of battle and recognizing the resulting heavy casualties, there are few details available about the individual attacks by the Skua pilots. Therefore, it is not known how many Skua pilots actually managed to complete their dive bombing attack and drop their bomb. Similarly, not known are those who may have jettisoned their bomb as they were blasted by the enemy fighters and unable to line up for their attack.

Before even beginning their dive, Dick's flight was attacked by two Me.109 fighters from the rear, one hit, striking Dick's Skua in the port wing. The only evasive action Dick could take was to skid with his rudder when given the alert by Richards, who was gamely firing back with his ancient Lewis machine gun. On their second pass the 109's hit his starboard wing and an additional 20mm. cannon shell blasted through the main gas tank located in the fuselage between the two crew members. At the same time Dick recalls a heavy blow, which he can only describe as being what a kick from a mule would probably feel like, as he was struck in his lower left side by machine bullets and shrapnel. Then, as the aircraft shuddered and pieces flew off, the cockpits became saturated with vaporized fuel from the punctured tank, which miraculously did not explode. Dick, in shock from his wounds, with blood seeping down his side into his left boot, vaguely recalls a third attack which seemed to miss.

The fighters broke off at this point, for their own self-preservation, to avoid being hit by the heavy anti aircraft fire now enveloping the Skuas. Scattered and badly shot up, the aircraft flew into the wall of heavy fire from the ships and shore batteries. Dick, now becoming faint and bleeding badly, attempted to keep flying his damaged aircraft. As conditions further deteriorated he suggested to Richards that it would be prudent for him to bale out, since the aircraft was badly damaged and barely controllable. Richards responded that he had unfastened his chute harness while trying to fight off the German fighters and doubted if he could get buckled up in time. Flying into what appeared to be solid flak Dick, although badly wounded, determinably commenced a semblance of his dive attack, released his bomb and although the aircraft was sluggish on the controls, and the engine running rough, he managed somehow to gain a degree of control over his stricken aircraft and shakily pull out of the dive.

With the crippled engine missing and vibrating badly, Dick, faint from loss of blood, desperately attempted to escape from the flak area by heading to the south, low over the water, toward what he thought would be the relative safety of the city of Trondjeim. This was an unfortunate delusion, since there he encountered unexpected danger as the aircraft was peppered with machine gunfire from roof top positions as he clattered, barely under control, over the built up area. A few miles past Trondjeim and barely clearing the terrain, his failing engine, now scarcely functioning, suddenly shook loose from the airframe. The doomed aircraft now virtually uncontrollable, momentarily reared up and flopped out of the sky and with a great shuddering thump crashed tail first into a small clearing. The loss of the engine probably saved the lives of both airmen since the Skua, without the weight of the dead engine, lost considerable forward speed, which greatly reduced the impact from the falling aircraft as it slammed into the ground. Dick, barely conscious, with Richards' help was able to stagger clear of the aircraft. Surprisingly the aircraft did not catch fire. Dick, bleeding badly from his wounds, was now weak and unable to move. Richards obtained a mattress from a nearby farm house and laid Dick out, who in turn gave himself a full shot of morphine from the syringe issued to each crew member. Being fully immobilized he then advised Richards to independently head over the hills for Sweden, which they estimated was only about 30 miles away. In hindsight Dick believes his bullet wounds were cauterized to a degree by the considerable amount of evaporating gas which had sprayed all over him from the main fuel tank saturating both his clothing and bullet wounds.

Almost immediately Dick was captured by German soldiers while he lay bleeding by his shattered aircraft.

Richards' brief dash for Sweden was short-lived, as he was quickly rounded up by two other soldiers who brought him back to the crash site at gun point. The immediate details following his capture are naturally hazy to Dick but he does recall hearing, with a certain degree of satisfaction, that his German captors were in a foul mood as they surveyed the overall bloody mess Dick left in the back of their staff car while en route to a hospital.

For Dick Bartlett and Lloyd Richards their operational war was over. But another and much longer and different war was to begin. Dick subsequently learned that the wreckage of his Skua, which had been quickly salvaged with Teutonic thoroughness, was subsequently paraded through Trondjeim as an example of what happens to British aircraft that have the audacity to dare attack German naval forces.

Dick and Lloyd Richards were immediately separated as Dick was taken to hospital. Neither of them was ever aware of the ultimate fate of the other for many years. However, in an interesting sequel Richards' family, who lived in Guernsey which was occupied by the Germans during the war, were never informed that he was alive and captured. Richards actually escaped from his imprisonment a few months before the end of the war and dutifully reported to the astonished Admiralty. There he was informed that since he had been reported dead for five years, the bureaucratic morass involved in bringing him back to life, so to speak, was so complicated, that it would be far easier for him to simply reenlist, which he did. So in a sense Richards had a 'second coming'.

The results of the Trondjeim attack were disastrous for the Royal Navy. Of the 15 Skuas that took off from *Ark Royal* that morning eight were shot down, including the two squadron commanders, Lt. Cdr. J Casson, (803 Squadron) and Capt. J. Partridge, (800 Squadron). Of those 16 crew members shot down, six were killed, and the remaining ten captured. One and possibly two hits were believed to have been obtained on the battle cruiser *Scharnhorst.* The Germans, however, admitted to only one hit by a 500 lb. bomb that failed to explode. Ironically, it was subsequently determined that particular bomb was inert, filled with sawdust and no doubt intended only for armament practice in bomb loading and handling.

There was a rare photo taken by Petty Officer Telegraphist, (TAG) Air Gunner Hart from the rear cockpit of the Skua piloted by Lt. Spurway of 800 Squadron at some point during their dive bombing attack. The picture clearly identifies the disposition and location of the 44,000 ton German battle cruiser *Scharnhorst,* four destroyers, a small cruiser and a large Hipper class cruiser anchored close to the Trondjeim side of the harbour. In the background the city is clearly shown, as is the small fortress/monastery island of Munkholmen.

As Joe Hill was to recount, the Blenheim fighter escort arrived unfortunately too late to accompany the Skuas. He said this became readily apparent while the Blenheims were still en route to the rendezvous with the *Ark Royal.* He remembers the Blenheim Squadron Commander accordingly later altered course directly for Froya. Indeed he remembers seeing one or two of the Skua attackers heading back to the carrier following their ill-fated mission. This incident was also mentioned by Dick Bartlett's surviving flight leader Lt. D.C. Gibson, later as Admiral Gibson in his 1990 Fly Navy article "Skua Strike on Scharnhorst". Quoting from Gibson's account, "About ten minutes after setting course for the *Ark Royal* from their departure point following the Skua attack, I was alarmed to see a flight of twin engine aircraft ahead. However, this turned out to be our Blenheim fighter escort, somewhat late. Pat (his crewman) flashed them on his Aldis signalling lamp and advised them to go home; had they gone on they would undoubtedly have been shot down."

By this time the Blenheims themselves were in trouble, due to the extended time they had already flown in their intended rendezvous with the carrier. Indeed there was considerable doubt by the crews whether they had sufficient fuel to reach their base at Sumburgh airfield in the Shetland Islands, the nearest UK airfield. Joe Hill recalls that they flew at maximum endurance power settings, finally putting down at the airfield in an abbreviated stream landing. Joe recalls that his total flight time for this mission was 7¼ hours, exceeding the official maximum endurance by an additional 30 minutes. When the fuel tanks were later dipped, the total fuel remaining in all tanks was less than 40 gallons.

Joe still has nagging doubts about the distances flown on the planned escort flight. The Blenheims had only recently been assigned to RAF Coastal Command and standard RAF aircraft instruments were calibrated in miles per hour for speed, and distances were normally measured in statute miles. Naval aircraft and RAF squadrons assigned for Coastal Command operations, such as the Beaufort, relied on instruments calibrated in knots and navigation was measured on charts using nautical miles. It is entirely possible that the 15% difference between statute miles and miles per hour versus the naval usage of knots and nautical miles was miscalculated. If this was the case, it would have considerably extended the estimated time (ETA) and distance flown by the Blenheims to the carrier's position and then on to Trondjeim.

Joe Hill had some other valid and interesting comments about the mission generally. First it was a desperate venture taking place during desperate times. Timing was critical and planning at the best could only have been 'ad hoc' due to the short time available. In addition, the constant surveillance flights of the RAF over Trondjeim may well have alerted the Luftwaffe that something was in the wind prior to the planned attack, and as a result the Luftwaffe was no doubt being maintained in a high state of readiness. The earlier than scheduled attack by the Beauforts obviously exacerbated this situation. Further, the aircraft used by the RAF were totally unsuitable for the assigned task, but nothing else was available.

Little information is available concerning the four plane bombing attack on Vaernes by the Beauforts. The RAF Air Historical Branch at the Ministry of Defence had only scant details of the role played by the Beauforts. Their mission has been compiled from these records. At 0118 on 13 June, 1940, a German heavy cruiser (believed to be the *Admiral Scheer*) was sighted by the Beauforts in a position bearing 252 degrees from Trondjeim at a distance of 80 miles. This position puts the warship close to the Norwegian coast a few miles to the right of the Beauforts track leading to Froya Island. It would also tend to confirm that the Beauforts would arrive over the target area perhaps as much as ten minutes earlier that the Skua flights. The Beauforts had to fly by dead reckoning over the sea, a distance exceeding 400 nautical miles, on a track to keep clear of the Norwegian coast before heading inland from Froya Island toward their airfield target. This made navigational accuracy difficult. Accordingly, a 5% error in timing was not unreasonable. The Beauforts' early attack on the Varenes airfield claimed two bomb hits on the south end of the runway, two hits on the barracks located on the airfield boundary and other hits among aircraft parked on the runway. German reports of the damage are not available. The Beauforts all returned safely to their base after an extended flight estimated to be about seven hours. One of the aircraft which had been hit by anti aircraft fire from Vaernes airfield crashed on landing, but the crew suffered only slight injuries. The Skuas arriving over the target at 0200, some ten minutes later, were accordingly utterly trapped in the intense attacks by alerted enemy fighters and the awaiting defensive fire from the ships and shore batteries.

In speculation, under no wind conditions, if the Blenheim fighter escort had indeed flown the entire planned mission from Sumburgh to the *Ark Royal*, on to Trondjeim, then back to Sumburgh, they would have flown a total distance of about 1,000 nautical miles. Their estimated total elapsed time would have been 6 hours and 48 minutes. If any headwinds existed or minor navigational errors occurred during such an extended flight over the sea, it is apparent that they would not have been able to carry out the full mission. Therefore, even if the Blenheims had been on time, escorted the Skuas to the target, engaged the German fighters and escaped, they would invariably have gone down out of fuel, ditching in the sea on their return flight.

If, however, against all the odds, the overall attack had been successful, the heavy German naval ships would have been denied their intended break out into the North Atlantic to attack the critical convoys to England, which was the Admiralty's worst nightmare. No doubt the Admiralty and perhaps the Air Ministry, in their wisdom, felt therefore that the high almost suicidal risk and loss of several aircrew and aircraft was justified during this critically desperate phase of the war.

Including the loss of the *Glorious,* her aircraft and aircrew, a subsequent study of Fleet Air Arm casualties in aircraft and airmen estimated that between 40-50% of the first line strength of the FAA were lost or destroyed during the abortive Norwegian Campaign. Shortly after all Skuas were removed from operational service and the fighter squadrons were subsequently re-equipped with more suitable aircraft.

Eighteen months later, on 26 December, 1943, while attempting to destroy a Russian-bound convoy, the *Scharnhorst* was intercepted by a Royal Navy force consisting of heavy cruisers and the battleship *Duke of York* and was sunk after an ensuing running sea battle.

RAF Coastal Command Beaufort torpedo bomber as used in the strike on the airfield at Vaernes.

Blenheim Mk.IV fighter bomber designated to act as fighter escort to Skuas from Ark Royal in attack on German naval force at Trondjeim.

Messerschmitt 110 twin engined fighter based at Vaernes airfield, used in attacking the Skua strike force on Trondjeim.

Me. 109 fighter

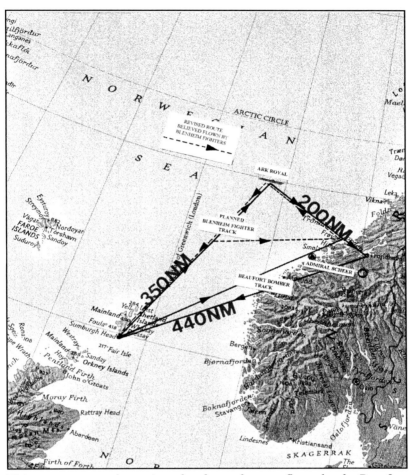

This map portrays the projected and actual routes flown by the Beaufort torpedo bombers and the Blenheim fighter bombers. Note the estimated point where the Blenheim escorts attempted to join up with the Skuas prior to their attack.

This range of 15 Skuas shows 800 and 803 squadrons ready for launching from Ark Royal on June 13, 1940, prior to their attack on the German naval force at Trondjeim. This is believed to be the only photo available of that ill-fated strike.

This sketch portrays the Skua strike approaching the entrance to the 60 mile long fjord leading to the position of the German naval force anchored in the front of the city of Trondjeim. (Drawing not to scale)

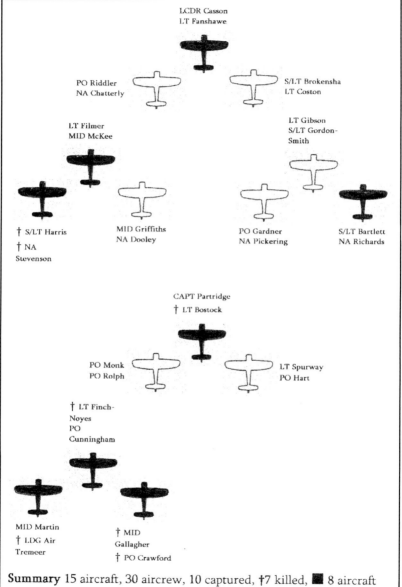

Summary 15 aircraft, 30 aircrew, 10 captured, †7 killed, ■ 8 aircraft shot down, 7 aircraft returned to carrier, 2 of which aborted their attack.

This painting portrays Dick Bartlett commencing his dive bombing attack on the German fleet units. Small red coloured silhouette on the side of the fuselage is that of an RCMP officer, denoting Dick's Saskatchewan heritage. Note three Me. 109s coming in for the kill in the background. Credit Dick Bartlett, painting by Colin Pattle.

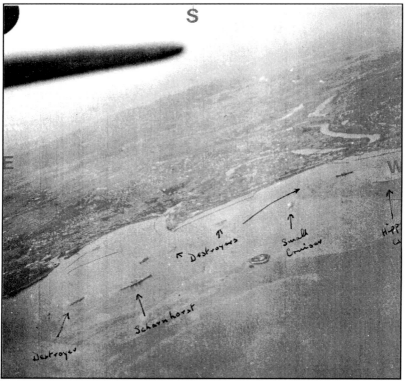

This photo by Telegraphist Air Gunner Petty Officer Hart flying as crew member with Lt. Spurway, identifies some of the German ships at anchor, with the city of Trondjeim to southward. The battle cruiser Scharnhorst is at lower left. In this photo the pilot is heading NW during the attack. This is believed to be one of the only photos available of this suicidal strike. Credit National Archives, Kew. Photo ADM 199/480.

German guard standing in front of wreckage of crashed Skua. Note the port wing has folded back and engine has broken away from fuselage.

Skua landing aboard HMS Ark Royal.

4

PRISONER OF WAR

An eloquent appreciation by Winston S. Churchill, written in 1899, portraying his sense of imprisonment during the Boer War, describes the precarious position in which a POW exists. This is quoted as follows: "It is a melancholy state, you are in the power of your enemy. You owe your life to his humanity, your daily bread to his compassion. You must obey his orders, go where he tells you. Stay where you are bid, await his pleasure, possess your soul in patience. Meanwhile great events are in progress, opportunities for action and adventure are slipping away; hours crawl like paralytic centipedes, life is one long boredom from dawn till slumber. Moreover the whole atmosphere of prison, even the most regulated prison, is odious. You feel a sense of constant humiliation in being confined, fenced in by railings and wire, watched by armed men, webbed about with a tangle of regulations and restrictions; one can only hate every minute of captivity." Captivity, however, under the currently victorious Germans would no doubt become even more harrowing and uncertain.

Dick Bartlett spent some time in a Norwegian hospital recovering from surgery and his bullet wounds. He recalls that he was treated well by the Norwegian staff, although the hospital was under control of the German occupying forces. As if living through an almost suicidal mission, being shot down and then surviving an incredible crash, one would think that Dick Bartlett's harrowing experiences were at least temporarily behind him. This was not the case because he narrowly avoided another disaster. While awaiting surgery to remove the bullets and shrapnel from the wounds in his left side, Dick vividly recalled that a German surgeon who was poking around the wounds mentioned that Dick's hip bone was practically sticking out through the skin. Dick then heard the dreaded word 'amputate' and immediately reacted by loudly remonstrating, then rolled off the operating table and walked around to prove his mobility and establish conclusively he did not have a hip bone problem. Fortunately, with the benefit of a 'second opinion', upon further examination it turned out to be a bullet imbedded near the bone just under the skin. This bullet and pieces of shrapnel were safely removed much to Dick's relief. Overall he was in hospital for about ten days during his convalescence.

While recovering, he had one surprise visitor, no other than the Luftwaffe pilot of one of the attacking Me.109 fighters. The German, who spoke good English, inquired as to the state of Dick's recovery, followed by a brief conversation in which the airman divulged that he had flown the German fighters during the Spanish war. It was not long before the officer brought up the main item for discussion, namely, would Dick confirm that his Skua was shot down by one of the attacking Me.109's. Dick readily agreed, noting in particular the fact that his aircraft had been hit by both 20mm cannon and machine gun fire, which certainly eliminated flak as the cause. Since he and his aircraft had also been struck from behind in an air to air engagement, ground fire was also discarded as the cause of being shot down. As Dick was ruefully to relate, the slow flying Skuas were pretty helpless as they lined up to commence their dive bombing run while facing the high speed cannon-firing German fighters, manned by pilots with considerable operational flying experience.

While Dick was in hospital recovering his strength his thoughts were directed to an escape attempt from the hospital, which was certainly less securely guarded than a POW camp. However, the only clothing he possessed was his hospital gown, which was hardly a suitable 'getaway' costume. His first attempt to obtain some clothes from the Norwegian nurses was not successful as they were obviously fearful of being implicated and punished by the Germans for assisting an enemy POW.

However, Dick learned that other less obvious anti-German activities were underway when later, in a casual discussion with one of the nurses, it was revealed that the third floor of the hospital was assigned to German soldiers who had been infected by venereal disease. The informant also stated quite openly to him that when any of the Norwegian prostitutes became aware that they were venereally infected, it was invariably their practice to delay reporting their own disease until they had made sure they had passed it along to as many Germans as possible. Thus, in their own way, the women were making their own individual contribution to the Norwegian resistance efforts.

Dick's second attempt, which he thought perhaps held more promise of success, was to enlist the help of one of the male hospital maintenance personnel, whom he assumed was a sympathetic Norwegian and would comprehend, from Dick's somewhat limited communication, that a more suitable garb was necessary for his escape. That Dick's message was successfully understood by the worker was not long in doubt, but supportive he was not, because shortly after an armed German soldier appeared and Dick's hospital patient status was abruptly terminated.

Since Dick's bloody and torn naval uniform, consisting of jacket and trousers, had been discarded, he was forced to wear a well used captured British army uniform, as did several other POW allied airmen. Next he was transferred under guard by train to Oslo. In company with him was a group of captured merchant seamen whose ship had been bombed and sunk off Trondjeim. These men were generally in poor condition and since they were civilians, they were not covered as prisoners of war under the Geneva Convention. Hence they had little or no status with their German captors. Dick clearly recalls one survivor sitting next to him who had a continuous pain in his head with a constant buzzing in his ears from the blast of the explosions which sank his ship. He was more than concerned how long the poor man could maintain his sanity under such conditions, which were further worsened by a lack of food and water for the previous 24 hours. At Oslo Dick was separated from the seamen and was confined to the Citadel, an old Norwegian prison.

Upon arrival there he was delighted to meet his Commanding Officer, Lt. Cdr. John Casson, and two or three other aircrew from the Skua squadrons who had survived the ill-fated Trondjeim attack. A few additional survivors, including Capt Partridge, had already been transferred to a German POW camp. None of the survivors were fortunate enough to have made it to the Swedish border and safe internment. John Casson was both surprised and pleased to see Dick, since he was convinced that he had been killed in the raid. Casson, as Squadron Commanding Officer, had already been asked to identify the bodies found in one of the crashed Skuas. Identification was difficult due to the condition of the remains, but one body was wearing a green sweater. Casson immediately recognized the sweater as belonging to Dick and assumed the worst. Sadly, Dick confirmed that the body was actually that of S/Lt. J. A. Harris to whom he had previously loaned his sweater. Although the group of pilots were thankful to see each other again, they were all painfully aware of the pitifully few number that had survived the strike.

Another airmen who subsequently joined the naval aircrew POWs was Pilot Officer Joe Hill, RAF, who had been the pilot of one of the Blenheim fighter escorts flown in support of the doomed Trondjeim mission. Joe, flying his Blenheim, had been shot down on 25 June, 1940, on a Norwegian sortie. He and Dick were to subsequently become good friends and today still remain in close touch with each other.

From Oslo the group of naval captives were transported to a ship bound for Denmark en route to a POW camp in Germany. During the day voyage the prisoners were confined to the ship's hold, but at evening just before sunset they were allowed on deck for some fresh air, while under guard by a soldier with a drawn pistol. It was when the prisoners were being escorted back to the hold a very serious incident took place which nearly resulted in a tragic outcome for the POWs. As the guard was closing the door to the hold he clumsily attempted to holster his pistol. Unfortunately he fatally shot himself in the attempt. Immediately armed soldiers rushed to the scene and for a few moments Dick was afraid they would all be shot as a result of murdering a German soldier in an escape attempt. Fortunately quick thinking John Casson immediately opened the door and boldly demanded to speak to the ship's Captain. Casson, who was an accomplished actor and the son of Dame Sybil Van Thorndyke, prevailed upon the Captain to hear the details of the accident. Fortunately, as it subsequently turned out, the two men had actually met in pre war days and in the traditional manner of trust and honour among officers, Casson's explanation of the unfortunate accident was accepted by the Captain and a nasty situation facing the prisoners was safely avoided.

After the ship arrived at Copenhagen, Denmark, the prisoners were held in cells overnight, and then transported by train in uncomfortable third class compartments with wooden seats, under heavy guard, to Dulag Luft 1, a camp in the Frankfurt area of Germany. There, at the Luftwaffe Interrogation Centre, they were confined for about 14 days until the middle of July 1940. Dick recalls that there was little interest displayed by the interrogators in the captured naval airmen since by mid-summer of 1940 Western Europe had been defeated and was now completely dominated and under the control of the Germans.

There was, however, one prisoner who had been at the

interrogation centre since being shot down eight months ago on Friday 13 October, 1939. This was Wing Commander Day, RAF, who was then Commanding Officer of a Hurricane squadron based in France. Apparently, at this early stage of the war, the Air Ministry were woefully lacking in intelligence concerning the capabilities and overall organization of the Luftwaffe fighter air defence forces. The Ministry's solution to obtain such important information was to have a Hurricane fighter carry out an extended 300 mile mission of surveillance of the known German air bases. Their instructions were directed to Day's squadron. Day, knowing full well that this was probably the most hazardous mission that one could be delegated, was reluctant to assign such a desperate flight to one of his junior officers, so courageously decided to fly the mission himself. The Hurricane, with a radius of action of about 500 miles, was certainly capable of covering a considerable number of German air bases. The problem of course was to accomplish this and to survive in order to bring the sought after intelligence successfully back. That Day survived the mission was in itself a level of success, but any valuable information he did obtain was obviously not possible to pass on to the Air Ministry. The Luftwaffe on the other hand obviously considered Day quite a 'catch', since first he was a senior permanent force RAF officer and secondly, determining the details of his intelligence mission in itself could be of considerable value to his captors. It was not surprising therefore that the Wing Commander had been held at the Intelligence Centre for over 8 months.

As Dick was to recall, it was of considerable concern to the new prisoners that Day's extended incarceration had involved him being treated with considerable leniency by his captors, even to the point where he and the Camp Commandant were socially very close. It was very obvious to the others that Day was being wined and dined to an excessive degree. The main concern of the other prisoners was that he may well over time have let his guard down and could be inadvertently providing his captors with valuable intelligence. The fact that Day had been held at the interrogation centre such a long period of time would tend to support this concern. Dick is quite certain that the misgivings of the other POWs had subsequently been made known to the Air Ministry through their own communications network, and the Wing Commander was believed to have been warned of the security implications possibly resulting from his special treatment.

In early July 1940, Dick and about 50 other captives were transported from Dulag Luft I by a slow train for two to three days under heavy guard, with little food or water, to Stalag Luft I, a POW camp at Barth on the Baltic Coast. At Bart, he was again re-united with Joe Hill and the two shared a room there.

Dick remembers a conversation he, Joe Hill and fellow prisoner Flying Officer Maurice Butt, RAF, had as they were discussing their unenviable situation and each ruefully describing the details of their last flight in which they were shot down. During the conversation Joe Hill mentioned that he had been assessed as 'above average' in flying ability. Dick then remarked that his own assessment was also 'above average' at which point Maurice wryly commented that he had been rated as 'exceptional'. As they mulled over the fact that although their respective flying skills were categorized at a level higher than most pilots, it had made absolutely no difference in the final outcome, because here they were sitting out the war as POWs. On the other hand, at least they were alive and the alternative of having been killed in action was not an attractive option.

As Dick was to comment, this was a pretty miserable place to spend his first confinement at a designated POW camp. The food in particular offered little sustenance and prisoner morale as a result was naturally at a low ebb. However, on one occasion Joe Hill recalls a lighter moment, when one of the less alert guards was unaware of the fact that one of the prisoners had surreptitiously impaled a potato on the tip of his bayonet. Thus so armed, the guard then arrogantly marched off much to the considerable amusement of the watching prisoners.

At this stage of the war the POW daily ration diet consisted of 2-3 slices of black bread, a small piece of sausage, margarine and a bowl of watery soup. Dick's introduction to black bread was hardly noteworthy, since, according to official records of the Food Ministry in Berlin dated 24 May 1941, it consisted of a recipe (for which there was little public clamour) containing the following ingredients:

50% rye grain, ie. cattle feed,
20% sliced sugar beets,
20% tree flour(readily identified as sawdust),
10% minced leaves and straw.

Faced with the foregoing diet, it was readily apparent that the resulting energy level derived was barely adequate to sustain health, let alone enough to actively participate an escape attempt.

Yet escape was always on the prisoners minds and the first tunnel began in late summer. This was a short-lived attempt, since soon after the tunnel construction began, the guards marched in and went directly to the tunnel entrance hidden in one of the huts. Since the POWs all knew each other by this time, the possibility of a German stooge passing escape info was discarded. It was decided it was almost a certainty that the Germans had installed microphones in the walls of the buildings. This was proven to be the case as they were subsequently located by the POWs. It was a constant battle of wits between the captors and captured, and with plenty of spare time on their hands the prisoners were always actively working on various escape plans.

There was one sad and unsettling incident that took place at Barth which involved a young officer, who had been a Swordfish pilot shot down one night at Dunkirk while conducting a futile attack on German positions. Regrettably his crewman had not yet properly secured himself in his cockpit and as the pilot put the aircraft into an abrupt dive, the luckless crew member was catapulted out of the aircraft and was killed. This weighed so heavily on the pilot's mind that he became increasingly despondent and remote. His fellow prisoners organized a watch system to ensure that he would not do anything rash. In spite of the attempts of his fellow prisoners to communicate and reassure him, the man became virtually out of touch and descended into a deep and utter depression. His fellow prisoners feared for his safety and did their best to keep him under protective surveillance, but this became increasingly difficult.

Although Dick had since been transferred to another camp, he subsequently learned much later that the young pilot one night broke a window in the block, jumped out, climbed up on the roof and began shouting imprecations at the guards. He refused to obey any orders to come down so was shot and killed. It was the view of his fellow prisoners that he had completely lost any interest in living and suicide was his deliberate choice.

There was an intriguing anecdote about one of the Barth camp inmates named Flight Sargeant Hall, RAF, who had recently been shot down in June 1940 while flying a Whitley bomber. Apparently before the war Hall was notorious for his poor punctuation when writing his letters. His wife finally laid down the law and demanded that she correct all his future punctuation mistakes before mailing. After the outbreak of war Hall, aware that any mail to his wife would undergo censorship, suggested that they could devise a simple code utilizing his proneness for failing punctuation. The genius of the method was its simplicity. Hall would insert a word after every punctuation mark. On receiving the letter his wife would take each word in order and when combined a coded message would result. Coincidently, in August 1940, the Red Cross arranged a special routing for POW mail to and from England and Germany. Hall then tried his code which was a complete success. His wife then took the code plan to the staff of the Air Ministry who enthusiastically decided to participate in the scheme. From this time on the Air Ministry would receive Mrs Halls proposed letters to her husband, edit intelligence information in the text and then Mrs Hall would sign and mail the letters. Eventually the Air Ministry, fearing the code was too simple, devised a more complicated version which involved the use of a German-English dictionary.

Although it was early in the war the Air Ministry, using statistics, calculated that for every 10 aircrew shot down, one would survive and become a POW. A number of aircrew were therefore taught the new Air Ministry code with instructions for any of those who were subsequently shot down, and if sent to Barth, to teach Flt. Sgt. Hall the new code. As Dick recalls, the codes over time were passed to all the POW camps and he does not think they were ever broken by the Germans.

There were many fertile ideas being developed to enhance the ability of the POWs to carry out their escape and evasion techniques. One in particular about this time was the forming of a special section at the Air Ministry known as M19.

One of their projects was to form a small company in the U.S.A. and in this way were able to send parcels to various prisoners from a variety of fictitious friends and relatives. The code in use would then be applied to indicate to the recipient that a special parcel had been sent. The designated parcel might contain an innocuous item such as a shaving brush. By hollowing out the brush a number of small compasses would be revealed inside. Another would be a gift of 52 playing cards and when each was split apart it would consist of a small map. When all the cards were assembled, a complete map of Germany was formed. Another example would be the gift of a game of Monopoly in which, when the playing board was split, would display a detailed map of Germany. In some cases even pencils, which were always in demand, would contain a small hacksaw blade.

Shortly after the tunnel entrance was discovered in the room where Dick was assigned, the suspect group of escapee prisoners were moved into the Forelagen. This was a special prison detention area outside the camp perimeter, located in a section of the administration headquarters for the camp. Dick now realized that his particular group was one that the Germans obviously considered to be potential escapees. Close attention would therefore be expected by the guards, particularly since the tunnel had been started in their hut. In Dick's case, his earlier attempt to break out of the hospital in Norway was obviously worthy of note. The separated group were therefore detained in the Forelagen to undergo a search before being moved to another camp. While being examined one of the men, who was carrying one of the previously discovered microphones, excitedly declared it to be a small bomb. During the ensuing confusion Dick quickly grabbed an already confiscated pair of wire cutters from a nearby table and managed to pass inspection without them being detected.

That particular night there was an air raid warning and all the camp lights were extinguished. Dick suggested to one of his companions that it would be an opportune time for the two to slip out of the camp. The plan was simple. One man, provided with a board, would hold the barbed wire up and off their backs, while the other (Dick), with the cutters, would be snipping through the tumbled barbed wire surrounding the camp. Dick reasonably thought that since the camp was on the Baltic, they could easily sneak aboard a Swedish ship and be in Sweden in no time. Unfortunately, by the time they were in the wire snipping stage, they found that the guards had not only tripled their numbers, but with dogs and flashlights they were also patrolling on the outside of the wire. To make matters worse, the 'all clear' sounded at this delicate stage of the escape. However, as luck would have it, there was a delay in the lights being turned back on and the pair were able to scuttle back into the hut in the nick of time.

As Dick Bartlett was to remark many years later, they were for the most part young and very inexperienced at the time. To plan an escape from a guarded prison camp is not the sort of knowledge that comes easily. Rather it falls in the category of 'on the job training'. Dick by this time was only 21 years old, but they were all expanding their knowledge and experience, with escape always the prime topic of discussion as the days wore on.

It is made clear to all serving military personnel that it is the duty of each, if taken prisoner, to attempt to escape and cause maximum disruption to their captors. The Geneva Convention in such a case does provide a degree of protection to successful escapees insofar as they cannot be executed if recaptured. The Germans conversely had the responsibility to ensure that their POWs remain confined. Since the land battle phase of the war in Western Europe was over for the time being, the recent presence of a number of allied Prisoners of War was a comparatively new experience for both prisoners and captors. Until the British army units, such as the 51st Highland Division, which held off the German army until the Dunkirk evacuation was successfully accomplished, there was not yet a large number of British POWs and their German captors had yet to completely establish a sophisticated system of prisoner camps and security procedures. Both sides therefore were in a sense in a learning role. The obvious loophole created by the Geneva Convention forbidding the killing of POWs was, however, fortunately still being adhered to by the Germans, so any escapees recaptured were still relatively safe from serious retaliation.

It was now January 1941, and the next day Dick's select group of POWs was moved by train to Oflag 9, located in Spangenburg castle, north east of Dulag Luft 1. Built on the top of a hill, surrounded by a moat with only a drawbridge lowered for entry, there was little or no chance of escape. First, although the moat was dry, there roamed within a large number of vicious wild boars, fed only on scraps and always hungry. Outside the moat were a series of heavy barbed wire entanglements. Added to these formidable obstacles, beyond the barbed wire were stationed heavily armed guards with searchlights. Fortunately, Dick was at Spangenburg for only about 6-8 weeks before he was again transferred to another camp.

.

5

CAMPS

The next camp Dick was sent to was Stalag 20A, near Thorne, Poland on the Vistula River, where he arrived in February 1941. This camp was a miserable, primitive, underground fort, one of the old defensive positions built by the Germans in the Bismark era to repel Polish attacks. The accommodation for the prisoners consisted of three tier bunks in dirty, damp, unused ammunition bunkers, with the only illumination provided by a solitary bulb hanging from the ceiling. The lavatory at night consisted of a bucket behind the bunker door.

As Dick was to relate, he understood confinement in this underground prison was, in part, retaliation against Canadian prisoners by the Germans for what they falsely claimed were similar conditions of underground incarceration of German POWs at the rebuilt heritage site of Fort Henry, Ontario, Canada.

Already in captivity at Stalag 20A were a number of British troops who had been captured at Dunkirk. They publicly swore at and generally derided the officer arrivals in front of their German captors. However, in subsequent private discussions between the troops and the newly-arrived officers, out of view of the guards, it was explained that this was an intentional ploy on the part of the British soldiers, who as POWs were required to be employed as forced labour. Their plan was to convince the Germans that the soldiers hated the officers and as a result would subsequently cajole themselves better rations than the new prisoners. Naturally the officers went along with the scheme and clandestinely received extra rations from their wily troops.

Dick recalls that later in the Spring the POWs were briefly permitted out of the underground area and allowed to obtain fresh air in the open area at the top of the fort. One of the first events he witnessed was the undisguised brutality inflicted by the German guards upon a group of civilian labour prisoners consisting of women and old men. They were assigned to dig a trench and were guarded by a few rifle-armed soldiers. One guard, however, was carrying a large bull whip, which he used to lash the prisoners as he walked up and down the line of workers. The group were obviously in poor health, suffering from a form of dysentery which necessitated them to frequently step away from the line. On such occasions Dick could hear their screams as the brute with the whip lashed the poor creatures on the bare skin as they squatted.

By May 1941, the Germans had began massing three armies, comprising 125 divisions, for the assault on Russia. Dick vividly recalled seeing immense numbers of troops, trucks, tanks and vast quantities of equipment moving east through Poland. For two weeks the movement continued unabated and the prisoners could hear the thundering noise of vehicles throughout the night as the German armies executed their invasion plans. Dick assumed this important intelligence information was being sent via the POW code system which, if nothing else, confirmed what was already suspected, that war against Russia was imminent.

During his confinement at Stalag 20A Dick underwent one unpleasant and dangerous experience. In this instance he had written a letter to an uncle in Canada and had made a point of describing the low quality and minimal rations being issued. This caused a reaction when the uncle publicized the poor food. Shortly after Dick was marched to an office in the camp Administrative Building and was treated in an intimidating manner by a small, insignificant, officious, but threatening officer, who promptly demanded that he retract the ration allegation and inform his uncle accordingly. Dick refused and was shortly after ordered to disrobe completely with his clothes confiscated under the pretext of examination. This was all part of the humiliation and intimidation methods the Germans practised on POW prisoners. Once again the officer demanded that Dick do as ordered. Again he refused. The situation became increasingly precarious as the German took his revolver out of its holster, laid it on the desk and once again demanded a retraction, which was still refused. Standing naked with no witnesses, confronting an enraged armed officer, Dick was now in a very precarious situation and feared for his very life. The next thing he knew the officer abruptly left the room and Dick feared the worst. To his surprise, shortly after, his clothes were returned and he was escorted back to his compound. As Dick was to disclose many years later, the German officer had been farming at Weyburn, Saskatchewan, in the 'dirty thirties' and had been recalled back to Germany before the war. His attempt to use this prairie farming background as hopeful basis for a common bond with Dick was obviously a dismal failure.

As Dick was to recall it was while he was at Thorne that he became involved in the 'medicine ball' caper. Through the friendly relations with Polish labourers at the camp, whose hatred of the Germans was almost a national characteristic, Dick and a select few of his companions bribed one of the Poles to sneak the components for a small radio receiver into the camp. When assembled, and by changing the coils, the radio became an excellent source of news from the various British broadcasts. In order to keep its existence secret the radio was hidden in what was described as a medicine ball used by the prisoners for callisthenics and sports activities. Under the careful control of a few chosen 'sporting enthusiasts' the ball was always kept closely held by the group, and as a matter of policy the only time the radio was not hidden inside the ball was when it was actually being used for receiving messages. Extreme precautions were always taken to ensure the ball was never dropped and always kept in possession of one of the group. This radio-equipped medicine ball subsequently travelled from camp to camp and became an essential continuous source of war news and intelligence.

In June, about two weeks before the invasion of Russia by Germany, Dick Bartlett and a number of other prisoners were sent back to Oflag 9A/H at Spangenburg Castle. This was an extremely arduous rail journey. The prisoners were not allowed to stand or move from the hard, wooden slatted seats except to use the latrine. Food and water was only grudgingly handed out in minimal quantities, and since the German rail system was designed with Berlin as the main hub the rail lines invariably went through or by Berlin.

The British night bombings of Berlin were now becoming more frequent in 1941, and Dick remembers that during such raids the POW train was assigned the lowest priority and shunted aside. Therefore, the prisoners transferring from Thorne to Spangenburg were on the train for an extended period, taking as long as three days to cover the 600 kilometre distance. He also recalls that the British night bombings were beginning to have a considerable adverse impact on the morale of the civilian population. This was not because the RAF bombings were intense nor much damage inflicted, but the fact Berlin was even being attacked was counter to what the German population had been led to believe by their illustrious leaders. The trip was particularly long and arduous for the prisoners, but they at least gained some satisfaction from knowing the Berlin bombings were causing disruptions to the German rail schedules and upsetting the civilian population.

At Spangenburg Dick was confined for about three months. It was readily apparent to him that he was now on the German 'Watch List', no doubt due to his interrupted escape plans while at the Norwegian hospital, his involvement in the abortive tunnel project at the Barth camp (Stalag Luft I) and the incident concerning the rations. The tight security at Spangenburg, coupled with the dangerous conditions outside the castle, obviously made any escape virtually impossible. As a result it was a particularly dreary existence as the prisoners were once again exposed to the strict security measures and generally primitive conditions at the camp.

In September 1941, Dick was again transferred to

another camp nearby, about 10-15 miles NE of Spangenburg. This camp was Oflag 6 at Warburg, where the majority of the inmates were the surviving army officers of the famed Scottish 51st Highland Division. This was the division that heroically fought in the successful rearguard battle at Dunkirk, thereby permitting the successful evacuation of the British Expeditionary Force. They had fought the encircling German army to a standstill, surrendering only when their ammunition was expended. Dick remembers with nostalgia what a magnificent group of men they were. Well organized and highly motivated, they had an active Escape Committee with a variety of plans on their agenda.

It was during this phase of the war, as the powerful German armies successfully thrust eastward to Moscow, that the rumours were rampant. One in particular, which came from the German captors, concerned the flight of Rudolph Hess to England earlier in May 1941. His mission, as seen by the German rumour mills, was to attempt a realignment of Germany and England and form a common military alliance against Russia. With this ultimate objective in mind the British POWs held in Germany were to be reallocated to prison camps in Western Germany. When the presumed alliance by the Germans was realized, the British POWs, which consisted mainly of army personnel, would then be in a position to reform into military units, rearm and take part alongside their erstwhile German enemy against the common foe Russia. It was for this reason that a number of British POWs, including Dick, had been transferred to Oflag 6, where the inmates were largely experienced British army officers. That he was included in this transfer may well have been partly due to the fact he was dressed in a British army uniform. Indeed, he recalls that many of his fellow prisoners invariably assumed he was an army officer.

Dick Bartlett was immediately made aware of the active escape organization. One attempt already being planned was a novel but simple plan to leave the camp by climbing over the perimeter fence. The idea was first conceived when the prisoners noticed that the electric wires leading into and around the camp were not insulated, and the power could be easily cut off by shorting the bare cables. Once the camp was in darkness the Scottish prisoners would then scale the fence with secretly constructed ladders. The plan called for the first of the escapees to be fluent in German, who then in the initial confusion of the darkness would issue orders to the guards to fire their weapons in the wrong direction, thereby giving the remaining prisoners the opportunity to melt away in the night. Dick had already left the camp when the escape was put into effect, but he subsequently learned it had been quite a successful breakout.

Although there were no successful escape attempts during Dick's confinement at Warburg, there was one very promising tunnel project that almost succeeded. First, it was proposed that the entrance to the tunnel should be located in the room of Group Captain 'Hetty' Hyde, RAF, one of the senior prisoners. He at once agreed and the chosen location was based on the assumption that the German guards would not suspect that a senior officer would become involved in such an audacious escape attempt. Since the snow was deep during the winter of 1941-1942, a shallow tunnel attempt was considered feasible and was now well underway. This not only saved a considerable amount of digging, but was virtually undetectable due to the snow cover. In order to have adequate ventilation to breathe while working in the tunnel, vertical air holes were pushed up at intervals to the snow level. This was most successful and allowed the tunnellers to progress rapidly toward the escape point outside the confines of the camp. As bad luck would have it, as the tunnel was nearing the camp perimeter, one of the guards happened to notice a column of steam rising out of the snow which was caused by the warm air escaping from one tunnel vent. The alarm was immediate! The tunnel was quickly detected and this escape plan failed.

A particularly bizarre incident that later took place had some unusual implications. A new prisoner had just arrived and was assigned to the same room in Dick's hut. He was dressed as an RAF Pilot Officer but was wearing a new uniform, and reported that he had just been shot down but had successfully parachuted. Always aware of the German attempts to infiltrate the prisoner ranks by 'moles' to spy on the POWs, the group in Dick's hut were immediately suspicious of the newcomer. Dick in fact had already had occasion to previously expose a German 'mole', who was quickly detected by his ignorance of RAF routine and squadron life in England. The prisoners concerns were particularly well founded since their room was planned to be the location of a new tunnel entrance, so naturally all escape activities ceased.

Their suspicions increased when the new individual's ignorance of general life in an RAF squadron was readily apparent and he was unable to give a good account of service matters. This, coupled with his rather unmilitary bearing and a rarely seen new uniform, promptly alarmed the hut inmates. The immediate result was to give him the cold shoulder and virtually ignore his presence. This treatment was obviously very difficult for the newcomer, but he quietly accepted the fact that he was an outcast with nobody to communicate with and as a result was virtually alone and friendless. In spite of this obviously deliberate and callous treatment by his fellow prisoners, he chose to accept their behaviour and in turn ignored them.

The ostracization continued and would have gone on endlessly had it not been for the arrival of a new prisoner, an RAF flyer who, when reporting to the senior British officer, disclosed that the Air Ministry was greatly concerned about the loss of a certain highly placed civilian scientist who had been aboard an RAF aircraft, that was shot down while conducting certain secret tests of a new radar prototype. There was deep concern at the Ministry that the scientist, who had insisted on personally conducting the trials aboard the aircraft, had been captured by the Germans and identified, thereby jeopardizing his highly secret research. It was with considerable relief that the Air Ministry received a coded letter acknowledging that the scientist (named Cundle) was safe, had remained unidentified by the Germans, and was now at Warburg posing as a low ranking RAF Pilot Officer. The coded letter used was the Air Ministry's expanded version of that originally conceived by Sgt. Hall as previously described.

From the scientist's perspective as a misplaced academic, forced to bail out of a crashing bomber, surviving the ordeal and being captured by the enemy, was certainly a series of unwelcome experiences he had neither been trained for nor had ever anticipated. This was particularly so observing his peaceful, academic background and his prestigious credentials as a prominent member of the scientific community. To subsequently be treated as an unwelcome misfit by his fellow prisoners was surely bewildering and extremely upsetting. He no doubt in turn, assumed they had become a small group of 'around the bend' and highly institutionalized POWs. As Dick was to relate, once the man's identity was authenticated, there was a general sigh of relief and the new member of the hut was made extremely welcome. Indeed, when his situation was clarified, he readily forgave his former tormenters for their unrelenting hostile behaviour. Cundle actually became a valuable member of the tunnel escape team, putting to good service his technical expertise in designing the installation of electrical lighting system for the tunnel diggers.

Dick and five others had in the meantime finalized their own escape plan, which had been approved by the Escape Committee. This attempt was to take place from the camp cell block, which was actually located outside the camp perimeter. It was common knowledge that the cell block was unguarded from Friday night until Monday morning. A key to the success of the plan was that all six escapees should be simultaneously confined to the cell block. This was not all that difficult, since by merely failing to salute a German officer was sufficient to warrant a period in the cells. A second important factor to the success of the plan was to effectively coordinate the actions of the group and distract the solitary guard. This was possible in a variety of ways. Although prisoners were separated and not able to communicate while in cell confinement, nor talk during their exercise period, signals such as stopping to tie a shoelace allowed essential verbal messages to be passed. Since at night the individual cells were secured with simple sliding bolts on the doors from the outside by the solitary guard, and the building corridor was dim and only illuminated by a single dim light, the group were able to distract the guard by banging on their individual cell doors and talking loudly or demanding to use the single privy.

Therefore on the Friday, as it became dark. one of the team returning to his cell was able to slide one of the door bolts nearly open on a previously selected cell so that in the increasing gloom it still appeared to be in the closed position. By repeating the process, and through pre-arranged signals and other distractions, a second prisoner returning to his own cell was able to slide the second door bolt of the chosen cell open in the same fashion without being detected by the guard. In the meantime, the prisoner within that particular cell would hold the door shut, making it appear secure.

On Friday night, since each cell had already been provided with a bucket for use as a toilet, plus a weekend supply of bread, the guard vacated the building and locked the guard room door, which was the only entrance to the building. The door bolts on the selected cell were then forced fully open by the occupant, who then released the other five prisoners. They now had full access to the locked cell building. Dick, who had shaped a small piece of metal in the form of a screw driver hidden in the heel of his boot, was then able to pick the lock from inside the building. Although the camp had searchlight-equipped towers facing the guard house, the team, moving in pairs, was able to slip away unnoticed in the dark. Dick does recall that as the time arrived for the escape attempt, he was forced to head out on his own, since his paired cohort was unable to walk for any distance due to a rapidly developing case of swollen feet infected from flea bites.

The escape was initially successful, insofar as the group managed to break out unnoticed by the guards manning the rotating searchlights mounted on the guard towers. Dick, however, did have an anxious moment when the circling light passed over him as he laid appearing as a dark object in the snow. One problem that soon became critical was the lack of food. To partially overcome this, the group had saved up some of their Red Cross packages and arranged for a foreign labourer to leave a supply of additional food in an agreed location for the escapists. Unfortunately, upon the team reaching the spot, the food was gone. Dick assumed that either the labourer had eaten it himself or else it had been otherwise stolen by somebody else. To make matters even worse, Dick was so hungry that he had already eaten his entire weekend ration of four slices of bread on the Friday evening, assuming the extra rations would be forthcoming as arranged.

His plan was to head west to Holland by hopping aboard freight trains at night, then lying low during each day. But by virtue of his inadequate prison diet of the watery soup and two slices of bread per day, he found it was totally inadequate to support any such physical activity and he was increasingly aware of his hunger and associated weakness. On the second night, completely exhausted, hungry and thirsty, Dick came across a small snow-covered stream. Here he ventured to take a drink and promptly gagged and threw up. The snow had also covered a large manure pile effectively polluting the water. By now, sick with the contaminated water and constantly vomiting, he elected to try travelling during the day. During the third day, weak and ill, and desperately trying to move from one train to another, he literally stumbled onto a small group of labourers under guard of an armed German soldier. Dick, in his British army uniform and obviously unable to account for himself, was immediately arrested. Bad luck also followed the remaining escapees who were also rounded up in a matter of days. They were in agreement, however, that at least they had the small satisfaction of knowing there would no doubt be punishment meted out by the Camp Commandant for the negligence and laxity in security procedures by his guards. After a few days in the local cells, and undergoing the worry of hearing repeatedly the dreaded word 'Gestapo', Dick was transported back to his camp at Oflag 6B.

Dick had another experience at Warburg which caused him a considerable degree of discomfort and pain. On this occasion, he was standing near his hut and noticed that one of the German camp army officers was walking in his direction. One rule in effect in the camp was that all prisoners must come to attention and pay their respects to any German officer with a customary salute. Dick used to avoid this demeaning procedure wherever possible and in this case pointedly chose to jump across a small ditch. He successfully avoided the salute, but found out that as a consequence he had twisted his foot and in the process had incurred a rapidly swelling and painful ankle. He stayed in the hut for a few days hoping his ankle would mend, but it was becoming increasingly swollen and he could barely hobble along. One of the more senior army prisoners examined the injury and it appeared to be far more serious than a sprain, so suggested that Dick have it x-rayed. The

Germans were not particularly co-operative, but eventually relented.

As it turned out, the x-ray facility was not in the camp, but rather a few miles down the road. Dick was therefore forced to hobble along in extreme pain, but the sadistic guard assigned to him insisted that he limp along in the muddy wet ditch running between the road and walkway whenever any pedestrian traffic appeared. This greatly increased the pain and to make matters worse, the guard would be constantly yelling at him to go faster or slower, depending upon his whim. Meanwhile, several Germans walking by and seeing the prisoner were openly showing their contempt by spitting at him as they passed. By this time he was so humiliated and angry that he nearly climbed out of the ditch to attack the guard. Sensibly, he knew that was exactly what the soldier wanted him to do, so rejected that action. Dick, however, did gain a small measure of satisfaction by knowing that the conduct of the civilians was their retaliation to the damage caused by the RAF night bombings, which was obviously having an adverse effect on the civilian population.

On arrival at the medical facility, Dick discovered that it was run by a religious order of nuns, and while removing his muddy wet boots attracted the attention of the senior Sister. After she realized the unnecessary brutal manner in which Dick had been treated, for what was determined to be a broken ankle, he recalls with a certain degree of satisfaction that the Sister gave the guard a good tongue lashing. He also well remembers the way in which she gently treated him and arranged transportation to take him back to camp. With insufficient diet and being generally run down, it took a considerable time for Dick to recuperate and regain his strength.

One very sobering and barbarous situation that Dick encountered was the murderous treatment of a large number of Russian prisoners, who were confined in the next compound of the Warburg camp. Dick recalls that, although direct communication was difficult, it was very obvious that the Russians were being treated in an abominable manner. During the winter months the British and Russians were able to send messages back and forth hidden in snowballs thrown in exchange to each other. Although the British prisoners were barely getting by on their own inadequate food rations, the Russians were virtually starving. Wherever possible, however, the British POWs would generously share their meagre rations or Red Cross food with the Russians. Although such opportunities were very limited, it was often possible, when the prisoners were allowed to use the showers, for packets of food to be surreptitiously passed to the Russians, to whom it was literally a salvation. It is rather ironic that the threat of a typhus outbreak in the camp was always on the mind of the Germans. Accordingly, showering and being dusted for fleas and ticks was a compulsory, regularly scheduled event. The fact that the Russian prisoners were starving to death was apparently not really of concern to the authorities, since starvation was not of a contagious nature.

The individual brutality of some of the German guards to the Russians was often most evident and they could be seen clubbing at random, with no provocation, any poor creature that happened to be in reach of their club or rifle. In addition to such sadistic behaviour, the Germans had their attack dogs at readiness and would release them at the slightest whim. Beaten, starved and frozen, the death rate among the Russian prisoners was horrendous. Dick wryly recalls that one morning, after a frigid night, a message in a snow ball from the Russians was relatively upbeat, since only five of their comrades had died during the night.

In one particular incident the Russians did, however, gain a small measure of revenge against their captors. This took place one night when one of the guards took his dog off the leash and the snarling creature ran into one of the Russian huts. This was a big mistake! The Russians swarmed around the animal who disappeared in the confusion and was never seen alive again. The next morning the pelt of the unfortunate beast was found strung on the barbed wire. The Russians meanwhile had sent a message to their British allies stating that the meal they had served from the dog was the best food they had eaten to date. Such was the desperate almost sub-human conditions that the Russians existed under, and their resulting high attrition rate was clearly most evident to their adjoining British prisoners. The miserable cold and monotonous winter continued, but as Spring weather arrived in April 1942 Dick was sent to a new camp, Stalag Luft 3, in occupied Poland.

Stalag Luft 3, located adjacent to the small town of Sagan, was an entirely new prison facility built in a flat countryside area north of the Czech border, with a large heavily forested area extending to the south. The camp was specifically built for the Luftwaffe to house the ever increasing numbers of allied airmen who, since 1942, as a matter of policy were deliberately being isolated from the POWs of the other services.

Luft 3 was complete with separate compounds. The

barracks were built on concrete blocks, each with its own kitchen and latrines built on concrete slabs. The barracks were divided into stove-equipped rooms. The camp was administered exclusively by the Luftwaffe and in the view of the camp commandant, Baron von Lindeiner, the camp was built at a level of such luxury that the prisoners would be so appreciative of their surroundings that they would not be inclined to make escape plans. As subsequent events will prove, the Baron could not have been more mistaken.

When Dick Bartlett arrived at Stalag Luft 3 he was assigned to the North Compound, which consisted mainly of British and allied airmen. There was a very well organized Escape Committee established and although his stay at Stalag 3 was of short duration, Dick was well aware that several escape plans were underway. No doubt since he was on a 'watch list', Dick was only at Luft 3 for only a few months before he was once more transferred to another camp.

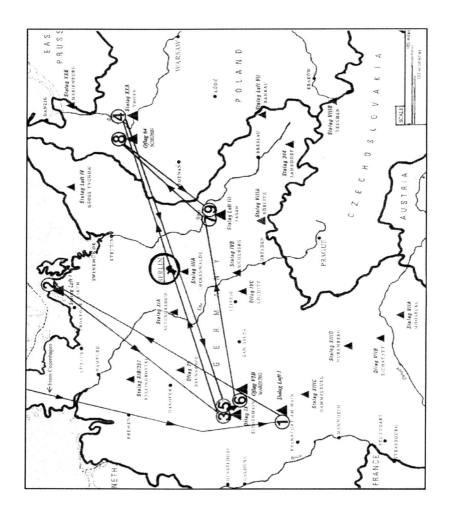

CHRONOLOGICAL LIST OF P.O.W. CAMPS IN WHICH DICK BARTLETT WAS CONFINED.
June 1940 - January 1945

1. Dulag Luft 1 Interrogation Centre: June 1940 - July 1940
2. Stalag Luft 1 (Barth): July 1940 - January 1941
3. Oflag 9 A/H (Spangenburg): January - February 1941
4. Stalag 20A (Thorne, Poland): February 1941 - June 1941
5. Oflag 9 A/H (Spangenburg): June 1941 - September 1941
6. Oflag 6B (Warburg): September 1941 - April 1942
7. Stalag Luft 3 (Sagan): April 1942 - Fall 1942
8. Oflag 64 (Schubin, Poland): Fall 1942 - Summer 1943
9. Stalag Luft 3 (Sagan): Summer 1943 - January 1945

6

OFLAG 64
SURVIVAL AND SUICIDE

This next camp was at Oflag 64 at Schubin, Poland, in the Fall of 1942. The camp was operated by the German Army. As Dick was to understand, it was the stated objective of the German Army administration to show the German Luftwaffe that the prevalent rash of escape attempts would not be tolerated at any camp under control of the Army.

Escape, however, was always a major priority at the camp and one tunnel was well underway. It had been designed to exit at a nearby Polish cemetery. However, the Polish workers, employed as slave labour by the Germans, advised against this project, as Polish cemeteries were considered sacred ground. Since their hallowed cemetery ground would be disturbed by the escape tunnel, it was their view that there would be little or no sympathy or support forthcoming to any of the escapees by the local Polish community, and in all likelihood any POWs, successful in their escape attempt, could well be turned back over to the

Germans. Therefore this project was abandoned.

As Dick recalls, there was subsequently a very clever escape tunnel commenced shortly after his arrival at the camp. The entrance to the tunnel was subtly hidden in the covered latrine building, which consisted of about 20 individual holes. By discontinuing the use of the first three positions and locating the tunnel entrance under the first hole, the entrance offered a quick start, and any German inspections in such unsanitary, smelly, surroundings would no doubt be circumspect in nature and not enthusiastically examined by the guards. This tunnel project proceeded well and by Spring of 1943 the project was completed. Dick later learned that about 40 prisoners broke out. However, to their misfortune they were all eventually recaptured, but if nothing else, it was a major distraction for the Germans, and since this large breakout was not the only successful attempt, it clearly showed the camp army administration that their vaunted escape proof camp has serious shortcomings.

For Dick Bartlett this was one of the most miserable periods of his long incarceration as a prisoner due to the fact he had incurred a badly infected wisdom tooth, which was not only painful but precluded his participation in any of the escape activities. To make matters worse there were no dental facilities made available by the Germans, which further worsened his condition. Finally, in desperation, a British Army doctor who had been captured at Dunkirk, offered to extract the tooth. This was of necessity performed with no anaesthetic or healing antibiotic drugs and left Dick sick most of the winter. With the poor quality of rations and his generally weakened condition, his recovery period from the infection was very prolonged and painful following the operation.

As a matter of record, the miserable daily ration in the POW camps was already in the process of being further reduced and by the of 1943 consisted of the following:

Bread - One fifth of an ordinary loaf,

Potatoes - 350-600 grams

Soup - One cup, (usually watery turnip)

Sugar - 20 grams,

Margarine - 15 to 20 grams,

Jam, meat paste& fish - occasionally.

It can be seen by the foregoing, that even if the ingredients were of good quality, there was very little nourishment to be derived from the daily diet.

Among the sometimes brutal and often shocking incidents that took place during Dick's period at Schubin, was one that was unavoidable and at the same time was almost predictable. This incident concerned the Air Force prisoner with whom Dick had originally been paired in the planned escape from Oflag 6B at Warburg, during the winter of 1941-1942. As previously related, this officer was unable to participate in that escape attempt due to the swollen condition of his infected feet. The two men met again at Schubin and Dick was seriously alarmed at the condition in which he found his friend. He was now in a deep depression and in spite of the efforts of his fellow prisoners his condition continued to worsen. In such a situation the standard procedure was to set up a continuous watch over the depressed man, to ensure that he would come to no harm. Sadly, his spirits continued to deteriorate and it was becoming apparent to his companions that the depth of his depression was now extreme. Haggard, weak, withdrawn and invariably bedridden, he had reached the point of unpredictability where anything might happen. The climax came with a sudden swiftness!

One day he unexpectedly arose from his bunk, abruptly left the building and before any one was aware of his intentions, he proceeded to walk directly and purposefully into the alarm trip wire surrounding the camp. This of course immediately alerted the guards who shouted for him to halt. Instead, he ignored the commands and headed deliberately toward the perimeter fence. He then came up against the barbed wire barrier and commenced to climb. He was immediately shot by a guard and mortally wounded in the groin. As Dick recalls, he was rescued from the barbed wire, gently placed in his bunk and mercifully died a few minutes later. Dick said that he would never forget the physical transformation of the unfortunate man as he mercifully passed away. All the haggardness and deeply etched lines of worry and fear in his face were completely erased and as the last spark of life was extinguished, he assumed a tranquil and completely relaxed appearance. So when death came, he finally gained the freedom and peace which he had been seeking.

Although the conditions at the camp in the winter of 1942 were probably the worst Dick had ever experienced, there was increasing optimism being expressed by the POWs as Spring approached. The news coming from the British radio sources, by way of the medicine ball radio receiver, was now very positive. The Spring of 1943 was being described as the turning point of the war raging on the Russian front. By March the Russian army had swept the German forces back virtually all along the front, and in some areas back as far as the starting line of the German offensive of the summer of 1942. The most significant battle occurred at Stalingrad, where twenty-one German army divisions were destroyed or captured, and by February 1943 all resistance there had ceased. This victory by the Russian army virtually ended the German efforts to conquer Russia by military conquest.

The hidden radio operated by the allied prisoners at Oflag 64 was in constant use, receiving the news from the BBC describing the disaster that had engulfed the German armies during this critical phase of the war on the Eastern front. As Dick Bartlett was to recall, the impact of this disaster on the German army camp guards was most evident. It was particularly so among the elderly guards, many who were former participants of World War 1. These men who, by and large, were generally more lenient and humane in their treatment of the allied prisoners, were now fearful about the outcome of the war and openly expressed their desire for hostilities to end so they could return to their homes.

By summer of 1943, the war news continued to be favourable for the allied forces, and there were even rumours of opening a second front in Europe. At this stage the German army authority made a sudden decision to shut down the camp, and with very little notice Dick was once again on the move. The medicine ball was now such a common object among the prisoners it became an accepted item of sports equipment, and in some instances the individual German guards watched with approval as the prisoners showed their dexterity using the equipment ostensibly to expand their athletic prowess. Accordingly, it was never questioned as an item of their personal property as Dick and the other prisoners were shipped back once more to Stalag Luft 3 at

Sagan.

At this stage of Dick's long incarceration as a POW, it is doubtful if any other allied prisoner had been transferred more frequently and experienced prison life in so many camps. Although he had been captured early in the war it was still unusual, and certainly suggests that the German authorities were deliberately moving certain prisoners more frequently in order to confine their escape activities to the minimum.

7

STALAG LUFT 3

N ow back at Luft 3, under the authority and administration of the German Luftwaffe, Dick Bartlett was at least relatively better off than under the often brutal guards of the German army at Schubin.

On his arrival at Stalag 3 in the summer of 1943, Dick quickly found himself involved in the well organized and active escape organization run by the POWs. Among those who now played a significant role as a senior director, was RAF Wing Commander 'Wings' Day, whom Dick had originally met while they were confined at Dulag Luft 1 in 1940. As a result of his considerable and ongoing experience with the medicine ball radio/communications procedure, Dick was asked by the organization to continue to provide the overall security and operation of the radio. With the greatly improved situation in the progress of the war in favour of the western allies, the radio as the camp's prime link with the British news service broadcasts was of increasing importance.

The properly designed latrines with running water at

Stalag Luft 3 provided an excellent secure location as a cover for the radio receiver. Accordingly, Dick and his team removed the radio from the medicine ball and cleverly concealed it in a most unlikely location, namely one of the toilets (henceforth not to be used) in the latrine building. A close knit group of three POWs was formed to provide the radio service. The first operated the radio, the second recorded the messages and the third (Dick) was responsible to securely hide the receiver under the selected non-operating toilet. After considerable practice Dick remembers that the whole communications procedure could be shut down in thirty seconds. In the event the radio was discovered, one additional duty assigned to Dick was to eat the received messages and destroy the radio coils.

The other camp POWs were led to believe that the function of the radio was to receive the regular BBC news broadcasts, but this was only a secondary function of the radio. On completion of the BBC news, it was Dick's additional responsibility to change the coils on the radio, then receive the coded Air Ministry messages. This was a risky but essential job, since such messages often contained important intelligence information of value to the POW Directing Committee and other key members of the prisoner organization. During the time the radio was in service it was never detected, although the German authorities were almost certain it existed. Dick remembers that the radio operator was an RAF airman by the surname of Ellen, who had been shot down in 1940. He was a big man, well over 6 feet tall and went by the nickname of 'Nellie'. Unexpectedly they had a great reunion when they both attended a POW gathering in 2002, not having seen each other since they were liberated in

1945.

There were a number of Royal Navy Fleet Air Arm officers now at Luft 3 as the various allied airmen were consolidated at this major Luftwaffe prison camp. In addition to Dick's fellow squadron members shot down at Trondjeim, there were a few other naval pilots including Lt. Tom Gray, Royal Navy who had been captured during the 1940 Norwegian campaign. Tom had the bad fortune to have been chased and shot down by a German bomber whilst he was attempting to escape after a bombing raid in his Skua fighter/dive bomber. Tom, a Canadian, had been in the pre-war RAF and was one of several members assigned to fly with the Royal Navy. He had subsequently transferred to the Royal Navy's newly formed Fleet Air Arm. A member of the same Gray family was Tom's cousin, Lt. Hampton Gray, RCNVR, who, while flying as a Canadian Naval pilot from a British aircraft carrier, was subsequently awarded posthumously the Victoria Cross while leading an air strike in August 1945 in the closing days of the Pacific War against Japan. By coincidence there was another naval FAA POW, Lt. Robin Gray (unrelated). He had been shot down in 1940 at Dunkirk while flying as an observer in a Swordfish attacking German forces. Although a pilot, Robin had bravely volunteered to fly as a crew member in the Swordfish. Sadly, Robin Gray was stricken with cancer while at Luft 3 and died before the war in Europe ended. His lonely grave identifying him as a Royal Navy officer came to light a few years ago in a remote Polish cemetery near Sagan in Poland.

By March 1943 the North Compound at Stalag 3, now consisting of over a thousand allied airmen, was a virtual hive of frenzied activity. Under the leadership of Squadron Leader

115

Roger Bushell, the Escape Committee had formulated plans to simultaneously construct three tunnels from three separate huts. The tunnels were designated with the names Tom, Dick and Harry and henceforth the word tunnel was never to be used by the prisoners. The design of the tunnels was a complex engineering project which required them to be 30 feet below the surface to avoid the German sound detectors buried six feet below the surface around the camp perimeter. A series of small chambers were built at the foot of each tunnel shaft to house an air pump, a sand storage area and a workshop. A major problem was the disposal of sand from the tunnels as the excavations proceeded. One ingenious method of disbursing the sand was by utilizing other prisoners called 'penguins' who carried pouches of excavated sand inside their trouser legs, then they walked casually around the compound distributing sand. At one stage as many as 150 'penguins' were employed simultaneously. The Germans, always on the watch for evidence of a tunnel, utilized a large number of their own men, called 'ferrets' by the prisoners. It was a constant battle of wits as the groups attempted to counter each others activities.

By August 1943 all had proceeded well with the three tunnels. 'Tom' had passed beyond the perimeter fences and had now reached the edge of the pine forest. An unexpected hitch then occurred, when rumours swept the camp indicating a new compound was to be added to the camp. This certainly appeared to be confirmed when German labourers began cutting away the brush to the west of the camp. This was in the area where both 'Tom' and 'Dick' were to emerge. With time running out, the Directing Committee decided to press on with 'Tom', which had been excavated at a remarkable rate and now had been extended to about 285 feet. As a result it would be necessary to close up 'Dick' and 'Harry'. The excavated portion of 'Dick' could then dispose the tons of sand being excavated from 'Tom', which had now exceeded the 'penguins' distribution capability. Indeed the 'penguins' had already had more than one close call, as in one case a 'ferret' had noticed the tell tale yellow colour of the excavated sand when he was idly kicking in the soil on the camp surface. Fortunately the tunnel still remained undetected in spite of numerous 'ferret' searches.

Unexpectedly, for some reason the Germans had zeroed on Hut 123 as being the source of 'Tom' and the 'ferrets' made a sudden sweep of the hut. In spite of repeated searches 'Tom' remained undetected. All appeared to be well until a 'ferret' picked up a pick axe left lying about by a worker laying a nearby drain pipe. The 'ferret', with hut occupants warily watching, began to idly bang on the concrete floor. As luck would have it, in a random hit he struck a corner of the trap covering the tunnel entrance and a piece of concrete broke off and the entrance to 'Tom' was discovered. All the work was for naught! The Germans were astounded at the complex engineering of the virtually completed tunnel and realized how fortunate they had been to have inadvertently thwarted what would have no doubt been a major escape of prisoners with the attendant problems of recapturing them.

Dick well remembers the disappointment following the loss of 'Tom'. Over the next few months a number of escapes by individuals and small groups were approved and attempted. Some indeed were partially successful as prisoners managed to break out of the camp, but they were all later caught and returned to Stalag 3. Here they were initially confined as punishment in the cooler (camp prison), located outside the main camp, the Germans optimistically but incorrectly thinking the caught escapees would see the error of their ways.

Things were relatively quiet at the camp until after Christmas, since winter was generally an off season for escaping. In January 1944, however, the tunnel plan was reactivated with the re-opening of 'Harry', the last remaining viable tunnel. From this date onward the North Compound once again was teeming with well hidden prisoner activity.

There have been several excellent accounts written of the escape tunnels excavated at Stalag Luft 3, but some of the information regarding this extraordinary enterprise bears repeating. 'Harry', as the last available tunnel option, was a major engineering feat. Although 120 feet of the tunnel had been completed, it was estimated that at least another 220 feet would still have to be dug to reach the protective shelter of the nearby trees beyond the roadway outside the camp. The disposal of tons of sand alone was a major problem, but this was accomplished by cleverly hiding it in the spaces of the tiered seating of the theatre built by the prisoners. Obviously, undue daylight activity at the theatre would have immediately attracted the Germans attention, so relays of prisoners carried out the job each night prior to roll call at 10 p.m.. By the middle of February another 50 feet had been excavated and by the middle of March 1944 'Harry' was virtually finished.

As the excavating had neared completion, the preparations for the actual breakout were proceeding at a fast pace. Tailors, forgers, cooks, map makers and instrument makers were all busy preparing clothing, travel documents, high energy rations, compasses and collecting or manufacturing suitcases for the planned escapees. Meanwhile electricians installed individual lights every 25 feet along the tunnel. The fact that the entire escape organization was conceived, implemented and the tunnel completed, in spite of the major German network of 'ferrets' and overall German high state of watchfulness, was an incredible achievement.

One of the key members who was very much involved in the tunnel design and construction was Canadian Flight Lieutenant, Wally Floody, who had been a peacetime hard rock miner. As Dick was to relate, Floody was mainly responsible for the design, construction of the shoring of the tunnel and shafts. After the war the two kept in touch and Wally Floody became involved in later years shipping rail car loads of daffodils from the West Coast to Eastern Canada for the annual cancer fund. He died a few years ago.

Since Dick had done such excellent work with the secret radio operation, he had already been approved as one of the prisoner escapees. Accordingly, he and a Norwegian friend planned to escape as a pair of Norwegian labourers and Dick was busily learning to speak Norwegian. However, shortly before the intended breakout, another Norwegian prisoner, Pilot Officer Nils Fugelsang, had arrived at Luft 3, who was an acquaintance of Dick's Norwegian friend, Pilot Officer Halldor Espelid. Recognizing that the two Norwegian airmen with their language advantage would have a better chance of evading detection, Dick graciously gave up his escape opportunity to the newcomer. In total about 250 prisoners were set to break out, which was to be the largest mass escape ever attempted.

Friday 23 March was selected for the 'great escape' and when the final layer of top soil was broken and the first prisoner reached the top of the ladder for a quick look, he was immediately struck with dismay. Instead of breaking ground and reaching the intended edge of the forested area several yards further, the tunnel exit was actually in clear flat open ground, barely 15 feet from a German sentry tower and only a few yards from the regular path taken by roving patrols.

It was now too late to stop the escape since the covering snow had now stopped and the exit hole would have been obvious the next morning. The rate of the escape was of course seriously curtailed as the prisoners had to wait for a clear moment when there were no guards in the vicinity. A coincidental allied air raid, did, however, assist in the escape process, since the power was turned off and margarine lit emergency lamps had been prepared to provide light in the blacked out tunnel. It was now becoming apparent that considerably less than half the number planned would be able to escape, since the rate of exit was only one every ten minutes. Just as the sky had begun to lighten in the east, and the next ten men were preparing to exit, a sentry practically stepped on a prone prisoner at the exit hole. Seconds later it was all over! 'Harry' had been discovered!

The total number of prisoners who broke out of the camp was 76. Three actually were entirely successful, avoided recapture and managed to reach England. Two of the three who reached safety were Pilot Officer Miller and Sergeant Bergsland, both Norwegians in the RAF. They travelled by train to France and were smuggled aboard a ship sailing to Sweden. Bergsland had a narrow escape while hiding in a dark narrow space in the engine room. German guards were thorough while searching the ship and one reached with his hand in the darkened space where Bergsland was hiding. The German actually felt the face of the hidden Norwegian but oddly, to Bergsland's complete surprise and utter relief, took no action and the ship left without incident. Bergsland later had a reunion with Dick in 1951, who was by then a LCdr. in command of an Air Group in the Royal Canadian Navy while serving aboard the Canadian aircraft carrier HMCS *Magnificent* on a visit to Norway. The pair had a great party not having seen or heard from each other since the escape from Luft 3 in 1944.

Of the remainder, five were escorted back to Luft 3, three were taken to Stalag Luft 1 at Barth, and five to a concentration camp at Sachsenhausen, Germany. However, in a shocking violation of the Geneva Convention, on the direct orders of Adolf Hitler the remaining 60 POWs were individually brutally executed by the Gestapo each with a bullet in the back of the head. The excuse given for this murderous outrage was that the prisoners were killed while attempting to escape. Dick's Norwegian friend and his last minute substitute were among the 60 prisoners executed.

Shortly after the mass escape, the Luftwaffe Commandant was replaced, and the Gestapo occupied and ruled the camp for a brief period. This was accompanied by prominent notices displayed in all POW camps to the effect that certain areas throughout Germany were now designated 'Death Zones' and any POW escapee found in such zones would be shot on sight. Since the Gestapo did not identify the location of the referred zones, it was obvious that any escaped prisoner would be shot wherever found. As Dick was to recount, the reaction in the camp to the mass murders and proclaimed 'Death Zones' was to say the least very sobering. As a result only an escape plan that stood a very good chance of success would be considered by the Escape Committee. After a few months, however, another tunnel was commenced. It was designated 'George' and the entrance was under the theatre.

It is worth noting that not all POW Luftwaffe camp commanders were prepared to obey the edict to shoot all escapees, as prescribed by the Gestapo decree. Still honouring the rules of the Geneva Convention, one Luft camp commander had the courage to circumvent the 'Death Zone' rule. When an escapee was recaptured, he dutifully reported that the individual had been shot as prescribed. In actual practice he exchanged the identity of a previously deceased prisoner, such as an individual who had succumbed to illness or other causes, with that of the recaptured prisoner. In this manner the escapee's life was saved, while at the same time the names of those "shot while attempting to escape" would be officially recorded.

On June 6 1944, the D Day landings took place, which was the news that everybody had been waiting for. When Dick and the radio team were alerted of the event from their coded message from the Air Ministry, the welcome news was only disclosed to a few key persons. This was to maintain the integrity of the radio communications system. Obviously, if the camp POWs were informed of the D Day landings prior to it being subsequently disclosed from the BBC broadcasts, their reaction would immediately alert the Germans that a clandestine communications source was available and being used by the camp inmates.

It was around mid July that Dick received a letter from

his father informing him of the shocking news that Chris, Dick's older brother, had been declared missing while piloting a Halifax bomber over France following a night raid at the marshalling yards at Lille. This was a major raid involving over 650 bombers of which 5% were shot down by flak and night fighters. Chris Bartlett, now a highly experienced and skilled pilot was Commanding Officer of 434 (Bluenose) RCAF Squadron with the rank of Wing Commander. He failed to return from the raid. Barty, Dick's father, in a letter to him had expressed considerable optimism that Chris, although reported as "missing", was still alive and hopefully under the protection of the French underground organization, which at this stage of the war was highly organized and had assisted so many downed aircrew originally posted as "missing". It was one of those fateful events. It was ironic that Chris, who had flown throughout the war, would be downed after D Day when the allies had complete mastery of the air and German night fighters, although still active, had been greatly reduced in effectiveness. Coincidently, Chris was downed on June 13, 1944, the same date that Dick had been shot down in 1940. Chris was on his second operational tour and had previously been awarded the Distinguished Flying Cross and Bar.

It was only a few days later that the tail gunner of Chris Bartlett's crew arrived at Luft 3. This was Flight Lt. D.H. Crawford of Port Arthur, Ontario. He contacted Dick and described the last minutes of the tragic mission. Apparently Bartlett's Halifax had been damaged by flak or a German night fighter, two engines were on fire and he gave the order for the crew to bale out. Crawford had just rotated his turret and was preparing to jump when a German night fighter collided head on with the Halifax. Crawford, by virtue of being located in the tail position, was the only survivor of the crew as the two aircraft exploded in a blinding flash. It was with deep sadness that Dick overcame his own grief and mustered the courage to write to his father and relate the sorrowful news that Chris had been killed in the collision.

After the 6 June landings and the rapid buildup of forces, the advances of the allied armies through western Europe was proceeding well. This, combined with the now seemingly unstoppable progress of the Russian armies as they advanced westward, made it increasingly obvious that the vaunted German war machine was beginning to crumble under the relentless pressure. Dick recalls that the thinking among the prisoners was that the next major challenge may well be their individual survival.

Among the German guards the effect of the tide of war running against Germany was noticeable by their behaviour and were becoming increasingly nervous and unsure of themselves, as the pressures on their military infrastructure increased. This in turn raised the uncertainty of the future of the thousands of POWs, particularly those scattered throughout eastern Germany and in the path of the advancing Russian armies. An additional constant worry was the unpredictability of the fanatical and murderous Gestapo and SS troops who had already shown no qualms about exterminating legitimate prisoners of war. In light of this, for many camp inmates this meant one could only hang on, keep your head down, hope for the best and wait it out. But the long days of boredom and unending days of hunger would only intensify.

Hallidor Espledid.
Executed after breakout
at Stalag Luft 3.

8

THE DESPERATE EXODUS

While the winter months closed in on Western Europe, the pressure on the German military machine intensified as the allied armies on the western front and the powerful Russian army offensive in the east continued. It was now becoming increasingly evident that an end of the war was in sight.

The situation of the 80,000 allied POWs was in many ways now becoming precarious. The first concern was what plans, if any, did the German military have to deal with such large numbers of prisoners. One disturbing and recurring rumour was that the POWs would become hostages, to be used as a subsequent bargaining tool. For this reason, as the Russian advance came closer to the Oder River, it was feared the Germans would do everything possible to prevent the POW camps from being overrun and rescued by the Russian armies.

For the approximate 1,000 POWs in the North compound at Stalag Luft 3, where Dick Bartlett was confined, there was little in the way of useful preparations that could be

127

made, due to the complete uncertainty and general hopelessness of the situation. It was indeed fortunate the Red Cross parcels were still coming through, which even though not regular, they were still a positive factor in helping to counter the bitterly cold weather in December 1944. By January 1945 many POWs, anticipating a move, began making what preparations they could, such as converting kit bags into backpacks, washing clothes, examining and improving boots, collecting socks where possible and hoarding, wherever feasible, some of the contents of their Red Cross packages. Some prisoners also began participating in walking exercises in spite of their overall lack of energy.

For Dick Bartlett, his own situation was not promising. Ever since his capture his clothing consisted mainly of the anonymous battle dress uniform of a British soldier. Although he did have a pair of army boots, they were in poor condition after four years of wear, and not able to provide much protection against the cold, wet winter weather. Unlike many other prisoners he lacked a warm greatcoat, after eventually wearing out a threadbare Polish coat. As a result, all he had for protection against the winter elements were extra sweaters and one blanket. Since the Red Cross parcels were inconsistent in delivery and availability, the occupants of his hut were unable to build up much of a reserve of food for any such emergency as a forced evacuation of the camp.

Further, strong evidence of the rapid progress of the unstoppable Russian armies as they battled further west, was the situation in the nearby small town of Sagan, which had mushroomed from about 20,000 inhabitants to an estimated 100,000, as refugee civilians began fleeing westward to keep ahead of the advancing Russians.

The persistent rumours of a forced evacuation of the camp were now beginning to sound like an ominous reality and by 25 January the Russian armies had reached the Oder River, only 46 miles east of Stalag Luft 3.

On the evening of 27 January, as many prisoners were awaiting news of a planned evacuation of the camp, a small group, including Group Captain Wray, RCAF, one of the senior officers among the prisoners, was suddenly interrupted when another POW entered the hut at 2100 (9 p.m.) and announced that everybody should pack up and be off in an hour. This announcement, coming in such a propitious manner and unusual hour, was an ominous indication of the degree of confusion and uncertainty that their German captors were now facing.

A stunned silence greeted this announcement. To have to move, presumably on foot, in the middle of a particularly cold winter with six inches of snow, in the black of night, was viewed as an act of madness. Individual preparations were hurriedly completed, but after that there was nothing to do but wait. First the Americans began their move from the South Compound, then two hours later the West Compound was evacuated. At 0130 on the morning of 28 January, 1945, the evacuation of the North Compound began which continued until about 3 a.m. As Dick relates, suddenly Red Cross parcels appeared and available for anybody that could carry them. One evacuee, Group Captain Wilson, estimated "at least 23,000 Red Cross parcels were left behind intact, and prisoners' belongings worth an estimated £250,000 were abandoned." Recognizing the starvation diet imposed by the Germans, it is difficult to understand the rationale of having hoarded so much valuable food, that it would suffice to provide approximately two parcels for all the inmates of Stalag Luft 3. As Dick well remembers, the intended distribution of a weekly parcel was seldom accomplished. Sadly, due to their poor diet, it was soon apparent that few prisoners had the strength to carry the very food they needed to provide essential sustenance and a degree of protection against the bitter cold.

As the lines of humanity formed up in the dark of night in the midst of a heavy snowfall, it soon became simply a matter of following in the footsteps of the man ahead. As the last prisoners left Stalag 3, Dick joined the rear of an estimated 10,000 men on a desperate exodus to an unknown and distant destination. To appreciate the scope of this mass evacuation, it was estimated that the line of 10,000 prisoners extended as much as 25 kilometres, straggling through what has since been described as the coldest winter in Germany in 50 years. Although most of the evacuees were young and reasonably fit, they were neither used to walking in snow and bitter cold, nor had the reserve energy to counter it. As a result, it was not long before the snow was covered with abandoned litter, including even some valuable items such as blankets, clothing and other personal items such as books, that the over optimistic thought he could carry, but had to discard.

After struggling for an estimated 17 kilometres with only a maximum 10 minute stop every hour, the line of exhausted men, after about five hours, reached the small town of Halbau. Efforts by the accompanying German officers to find some accommodation were fruitless. So the trek continued and it was almost better to move than stand in the cold. The nearest town was now Freiwaldau, 14 kilometres away. Makeshift sleds carrying food and other personal items began falling apart and the weakened prisoners did not have the strength to pick up these items which were left lying in the snow. As the column straggled through small villages, the local inhabitants were generally quite sympathetic, and if part of the column stopped at a village, sometimes hot water would be made available for the cold, hungry, energy-drained men to make some coffee.

After eight hours of trudging through the snow and bitterly cold wind, some now could no longer keep up and fell out to the rear of the column. Dick recalls seeing some of these unfortunate individuals lying by the wayside. Others, scarcely able to take one step after the other, struggled back to reach the rear of the line in the belief that horse drawn sleds or open carts were available to those who could no longer continue.

It was Dick's understanding, however, that any transport located at the end of the column was intended exclusively to provide food and transport for the accompanying guards. He also recalls at that time the ominous warning by the accompanying guards, that any prisoner who dropped out of the column would be shot. He definitely remembers seeing snow-covered mounds on the sides of the column which he firmly believes were some of those who literally just gave up, fell by the wayside and froze to death. In this regard there has never been an accounting or verification of the numbers of POWs who died during this terrible ordeal. There is no verification that an accurate German record of names and number of prisoners on the trek, including those in the lost and sick category, was ever compiled. As a matter of interest, in Dick Bartlett's own case, in 1999 he attempted to have his summary as a Royal Navy officer POW in Germany made available to him through the appropriate service channels. When the answer finally came back, he was mystified to learn that no such information could be found from a search of German records. One can only speculate that if an allied officer can be held prisoner for nearly five years with no documentation of his imprisonment, how many other POWs, who failed to survive the ordeal for various reasons, just simply ended up in the category of missing or having died while in captivity.

About noon the head of the column reached the small town of Freiwaldau, and it must have been an unnerving sight for the residents as the town square was filled with the ragged, shivering, sodden, hungry and thirsty prisoners. In addition was the ever increasing number of civilian refugees fleeing from the advancing Russian armies. In spite of this, some local inhabitants did their best, wherever possible, by handing out hot water with sympathetic smiles. Some of the prisoners tried to bribe their way, exchanging cigarettes for accommodation, but this was fruitless as the already entrenched German military personnel in the various inns bundled them back out in the cold. It soon became obvious that any plan to billet the POWs at Freiwaldau was doomed to failure, due to the massive number of previously arrived refugees. The German major in command of the North Compound column, overruled by the objections of the local military authority, was forced to continue with the trek and head for Lieppa, the next hamlet six kilometres further on.

From several accounts the final six kilometres was a terrible ordeal. After standing helplessly in the cold wind many of the prisoners began to freeze as their sweaty, sodden clothing had solidified to ice during the wait. At 1730, after a painfully slow progress, the utterly exhausted men managed to reach Lieppa, where approximately 1,000 prisoners were herded into two barns. After 16 hours of trudging through the icy wind and deep snow over a distance of 16 kilometres, even an unheated hay barn was a welcome respite. Numb from exposure, unfed except for possibly a few biscuits, their remaining food frozen, many of the POWs had reached the point where their strength had been drained and they did not even have the energy to worry about freezing to death. With an estimated 400 men in one barn and 600-700 in the other, with neither water nor latrine facilities available, the living conditions were horrendous. By now many individuals were already suffering from dysentery and vomiting from having choked down their ice-covered bread and tinned food.

At 0830, 29 January, 1945, after the German guards had made a failed attempt to conduct a prisoner count, the tortuous trek continued in the freezing cold. Not counting the sick who had left the column, several groups of prisoners now organized themselves by conducting their own head count by the number of individuals who walked together. By noon the column had reached Priebus and had a break for 'lunch', which consisted primarily of a few frozen or soggy biscuits washed down by water provided to a fortunate few by some of the more generous local inhabitants. Fortunately the German authorities gave the prisoners a respite at Priebus and 30 January was spent there, providing an opportunity to partially recover from the miserable ordeal of the previous 48 hours.

On 31 January, the column once more got underway

and after struggling through the entire day the column finally reached the small town of Muscau at 1800. Here for the first time there appeared to be an attempt to establish some order by the Germans, as they arranged a variety of accommodation, which included a cinema, riding school, stable, laundry, a pottery and a former French POW camp. One party in the last group to arrive were actually marched a further two miles to a glass factory. Here, much to their pleasant surprise, they were made welcome in an office with a fireplace. For the first time these few were able to dry their clothes and thaw out their frozen Red Cross food and boil water. Hundreds of others were not so fortunate as unsanitary conditions finally developed into a major dysentery outbreak.

On 1 February, after reorganizing and forced to abandon whatever was unnecessary, just keeping the essentials, the column restarted in late afternoon and set off for the town of Spremberg. A few prisoners, who were able to hoard some of their precious parcels, managed to barter their supply of cigarettes for food. Although the cold weather had abated somewhat, the attempt to walk in slush was not much better, and as night came the slush turned to ice. A number of the less fortunate now had severe frostbite and were unable to wear their boots, forcing them to struggle along in stocking feet. This, in addition to the severe effects of the earlier marches and the unwilling Germans to have regular stop and rest periods, turned this stage of the journey into a nightmare. Now the situation had deteriorated even further as thousands of men trudged through the night, many of them ill with stomach cramps and recurring attacks of nausea accompanied with diarrhea. The trek continued all night long, with each prisoner issued only a quarter of a loaf each of the sawdust-laden German bread for sustenance. It was not until 1400, 2 February, that the prisoners reached Spremberg. Here they were temporarily accommodated at the reserve depot of the 8th Panzer Division. This stop was for only a two hour respite and an issue of watery soup and hot water. The column once again reformed and plodded to a train station, a further distance of four kilometres. By now the numbers in the column had been considerably reduced, as many of the RAF and American aircrew prisoners had been sent on to other camps after arrival at Priebus and Muskau.

There was no doubt in Dick's mind that the ordeal of struggling through the snow was the worst he had ever experienced, and indeed years later he often wondered how he had even survived those desperate days of the forced evacuation. It was also remarkable how some of the prisoners, although terribly weakened, were able to assist others in even worse condition during the ordeal, not only sharing the burden of carrying the individual packs of essential food, but in some cases sharing in the burden of carrying those who were too weak to continue.

One such example was FAA pilot, Sub Lt. John Nicholson. He was shot down flying a Swordfish over Dunkirk in 1940 attempting to slow the German offensive armed only with the pitiful armament of bombs and guns carried by the obsolete aircraft. This was a good indication of how desperate the British were as they attempted to evacuate the British army. Nicholson had been wounded in the action, and although unaware of it the bullet remained lodged close to his heart, a dangerous situation for one under such duress. He credits Dick Bartlett with saving his life, as he was so exhausted at times, as he struggled though the bitter weather, that he just wanted to stop and lie down in the snow. Dick half carrying and by continuous cajoling forced Nicholson to 'hang on and keep going', was thus able to keep him on his feet as the weary column wended its way along the tortuous trail, seemingly travelling nowhere. Dick also recalls that during one rest stop he was forced to loosen the laces on his boots to relieve the intense pain of his swollen feet. When it was time to resume the trek his hands were so numb that he could not even tie the boot laces. John in this case was luckily able to tie the laces for him, which Dick claims enabled him to continue shuffling along.

It was only later, following his liberation, when John Nicholson was being given his medical, that the bullet was found imbedded within an inch of his heart. It was too risky to attempt to remove the bullet, so John was discharged from the service medically unfit with a miserly pension of a few pounds per month. After the war the two men continued their friendship and indeed John Nicholson visited Dick in 1946, and at his invitation later that year John spent Christmas with the Bartlett family at Fort Qu'appelle. Here he met Dick's family and indeed married Dick's sister Dora a year later on 30 December, 1947. John Nicholson subsequently became a well known academic at Cornell University, followed by Harvard, where he received his degree of Doctor of Business Administration He later became Associate Dean at the University, where he remained active until his death in 1980. The bullet was never removed.

The remainder of the column, after straggling into the train station, were surrounded by guards and then herded and prodded like animals into cattle cars. As many as 45 men were jammed into each car, which was already filthy with both human and bovine excrement. The sick stretched out on the floor, but as the train clattered and swayed through the cold night, those who remained standing were too exhausted to remain upright and soon all had slumped to the floor, wedged together in the stinking, cramped, swaying car. As Dick Bartlett was to comment many years later, even animals being transported to the slaughter houses were given better treatment.

By the morning of 3 February, the situation in the cars was horrific, the air foul with the stench of vomit and the results of dysentery. In one car the occupants managed to tear part of a board off the floor gaining a small access to get rid of the excrement and vomit. Later, after arriving at Halle that night, the prisoners were faced with another disastrous setback, as upon their arrival the field kitchen that was supposed to be feeding the train prisoners was completely bare of food. It had been consumed by the occupants of a hospital train that had stopped earlier heading west from the Eastern front. The prisoners remained without food and water for another 24 hours until the train finally reached the outskirts of Hanover early on the morning of 4 February. It was here that the German officer in charge of the prisoners, recognizing their serious predicament, allowed them all to vacate the rail cars and beg some water from the adjacent houses. This was the first water obtained since leaving the town of Spremberg 36 hours before. By this time the prisoners were filthy dirty, wet, reeking of excrement and vomit, and many so ill they could barely stand let alone make an attempt at walking.

Back again in the cars, by the evening of 4 February the train arrived at Tarnstedt, about 25 kilometres north-east of Bremen. Here the Luftwaffe guards were replaced by German army guards. Once again the prisoners vacated and formed up in a shuffling, wavering column and trudged another four kilometres to the next camp, which was identified as Marlag/Milag, where previously merchant navy prisoners of war had been confined. Although the first of the column had reached the camp at about 1900, by the time individual indoctrination and personal searches had been made of all the prisoners, it was not until about 0200 on the morning of 5 February that the last of the column had been processed. The camp had already been officially condemned for occupancy, due in part to the fact that upon their departure, the merchant navy prisoners had ransacked the buildings because they had heard it was going to be re-occupied with German personnel, presumably refugees.

Although the accommodation was rat infested, damp and smelly, it was a relative luxury after the miserable experience of the last 10 days. The buildings were divided into rooms with the familiar bunk beds, but no bedding was provided other than a pile of straw or damp wood shavings. There were stoves provided in each room, but neither wood nor coal was available. Later, however, the German guards permitted small groups of prisoners to forage in the nearby fields and woods for fuel. Although these forays were not particularly successful, it was the first taste of freedom outside the camp confines where those involved were escorted with but a single guard. Just smelling the clean country air and feeling the warmth of the occasional spring sun was a tonic in itself.

Unfortunately the general health of the prisoners after their week of deadly trekking was particularly bad. In addition, the fact that the flow of Red Cross parcels over the past six months had often been at half the normal entitlement, was certainly a contributing factor. As a result, it was estimated that about 70% of the prisoners were suffering from a variety of illnesses, including exhaustion, gastritis, frostbite, dysentery, cold, influenza and other various ailments which could only be treated in a rudimentary fashion by the hospital staff.

Although the physical condition of the prisoners was poor, at this stage of the war instructions had been given to forego any escape attempts, since the allies in the west were rapidly approaching the Rhine. Recognizing the close proximity of the armies closing in from the west, it was obvious that the camp would have to be evacuated or else the prisoners would soon be liberated. Accordingly, hoarding essentials such as food was a priority, as well as cigarettes, coffee, soap and chocolate, all of which had a great bartering value. As the days slowly passed the general health of the prisoners began to improve, and with better weather in the offing morale showed a marked improvement.

On 1 March, the camp faced another in a series of cutbacks in the individual food allowance, as the bread ration was reduced to 1/7 of a loaf per day with a corresponding reduction in the margarine and sausage ration. It was a blessing that the Red Cross parcel allowance began to arrive on a more consistent basis and the extended period of rain and snow finally broke on 8 March. After five weeks of rain and snow the sun appeared, which further raised the spirits of the camp inmates.

With the benefit of a hidden radio receiver the war news continued to be a constant source of optimism, and later in March a large scale night raid by the RAF, involving 1,250 aircraft, was reported with only 13 aircraft being shot down. Another raid in daylight by US Fortresses and Liberators, estimated to number about 850 aircraft, flew apparently unmolested over the camp. The most recent news that the allies had crossed the Rhine was warmly applauded, but it also raised the fears that another forced trek might be pending. On 23 March the prisoners were suddenly made aware of the sound of familiar aircraft engines and beheld about 120 RAF Lancaster bombers passing over the camp as they lined up for a bombing run on nearby Bremen. Large scale RAF bombing raids, which had previously only been conducted at night, were now being carried out in daylight, further strengthened the belief that the German air defences were largely ineffective and the end of the war must be near.

As March passed the rumours increased of a pending evacuation eastward to avoid the allied advances, and on 9 April the order came to evacuate the compound at 1800. The order was later rescinded after a false start at 2000. The evacuation was rescheduled for the next morning, 10 April. With the intervention of Group Captain Wray, a senior prisoner, the German commandant agreed to a more leisurely pace of about two kilometres per hour. At 1100 the column got underway, reaching the village of Zeven at 1800, and after a short rest arrived at Hesslington, where the night was spent in an open, damp field. One incident which provoked a considerable amount of anger was the deliberate shooting of two prisoners in the legs by a guard as a small number of prisoners went over the adjacent fence to collect straw for mattresses from nearby haystacks. The furore this caused was gradually lessened as the German commandant ordered the guilty guard to be jailed and the wounded pair taken to the nearest hospital. This action by the German commander indicated conclusively that the end of hostilities was fast approaching and any mistreatment of prisoners would not be condoned.

On 11 April the move re-commenced about noon and continued at the same leisurely pace. However, in the afternoon a sad and unnecessary incident took place when the rear of the column, composed mainly of Royal Navy officers, was strafed by an RAF fighter, killing three and wounding four. Dick Bartlett clearly remembers this sad and needless event. With the war virtually over and freedom for the POWs at hand, it was tragic for those men to die at the hands of 'friendly fire' after surviving the years of hardship and mistreatment during their incarceration.

As Dick was later to relate, he did succeed in gaining a measure of personal satisfaction for past mistreatment over the years, when during this strafing attack prisoners and guards alike fled from the open road to the marginal safety of the ditches. Dick, correctly assuming that he would not be recognized in the confusion, ended up jumping into the ditch deliberately landing heavily with both boots on a prone guard.

At about 1800 the column arrived at Bokol. Here the carefully hoarded coffee, soap and chocolate was traded with the inhabitants. Prams and anything with wheels were particularly sought after by the prisoners, similarly the supply of scarce items offered by the prisoners was in great demand by the German housewives. The column camped once again in an open field for the night.

Thursday 12 April, the prisoners had a surprisingly

welcome announcement following a long period for lunch, when the Commandant declared a 24 hour rest break about two kilometres outside Harsefelt. Also, by this time the guards were considerably more relaxed and appeared to be anxious to blend in with the prisoners, some of them even allowing their rifles to be carried in the makeshift carts which were being pushed along. Buoyed with the good weather now prevailing, morale overall was relatively high as the prisoners relaxed, gathered wood and enjoyed a surprisingly nourishing lunch of meat and bread. Trading also continued unabated, with local wheelbarrows being avidly exchanged by the German inhabitants.

On 13 April the column restarted and that night camped on the banks of the River Elbe not far from Hamburg. The next day they crossed the river to Blankenese, then on to Sulldorf with rumours that the destination of the column was Lubeck, near the Baltic Sea. The latest war news also reported that the allies were now only 76 miles southwest of Hamburg, this no doubt accounting for the increasingly casual and benign attitude of the guards who appeared to have already surrendered, at least in spirit. 'Bartering' and 'marketing' was the evening activity by many of the column and precious eggs were eagerly traded with the local farmers.

There was one unusual but memorable event that took place about this time which Dick Bartlett will always remember. As he recalls, his ragged group in the column was straggling wearily, dirty and hungry, somewhere on the outskirts of Hamburg, and as they moved slowly along Dick noticed a well dressed, middle-aged, German woman approaching from the opposite direction. Clearly afraid of the guards, and in order that they would not notice her actions, she continued to look straight ahead and without turning her head to look at the prisoners, she spoke clearly in English and said, "I don't know who you are and I don't know where you are going, but I wish you Good Luck!"

Days later as the column straggled at a leisurely pace toward Lubeck, the sounds of battle were increasingly obvious, with the noise of aircraft passing overhead and artillery fire clearly heard in the distance. On 17 April, after passing through the village of Ellerback, the prisoners came to a halt and here the sick and lame were separated, and rather surprisingly transport appeared to take them to Lubeck. Restarting on 19 April, the column entered the town of Garsted, and with the now casual control being exercised by the guards the prisoners were dispersed in the main street for lunch, which in some cases was augmented with bartered eggs being exchanged by the prisoners for a can of coffee. As Dick was to relate, the attitude of the German population had completely changed. Now long gone was the hostile and contemptuous expressions experienced in the past, and it was readily apparent that currying favour with the prisoners was the first priority, be it by bartering or sharing a meal in a farm kitchen. It is worth mentioning that such a meal was usually followed by a request for a written note from the individual prisoner expressing his appreciation for the kind treatment received. By 20 April the progress being made by the column continued to be relaxed, and after a 14 kilometre walk the prisoners reached Elhemhorst. The allies were now reported to be only about 30 kilometres away at Harburg, a few kilometres south east of Hamburg. Further to the east the noose was steadily being tightened with the capture of Leipzig and Magdeburg by the western allies. There was a general optimistic feeling by the prisoners that the column may well be intercepted from the west by the allies before reaching Lubeck.

On 21 April a 24 hour halt was given and those that wished to find improved accommodation were allowed to do so. Some prisoners were fortunate to find a nearby dairy where unexpectedly hot showers were available. By now Lubeck was only 28 kilometres ahead and with the relaxed discipline in effect a number of prisoners elected to press on to their destination. As Robert Buckham writes in his book 'Forced March to Freedom', a group of prisoners arrived at the village of Neritz where, to their delight, the owner of a small inn was more than pleased to cook an omelet if the eggs could be supplied by the prisoners. After the meal the group planned on setting out for Lubeck, but a caution from the innkeeper's wife alerted the prisoners that the local SS were rounding up any POWs who had preceded the column. This was a timely warning and sure enough they barely had time to hide before an armed trooper stalked by with his automatic rifle at the ready. A second meal was therefore prepared at the inn that evening. On the morning of 22 April Buckham's group was presented with a breakfast of eggs and coffee, rejoined the advance group of the column and resumed the march covering a distance of 16 kilometres toward Lubeck.

At this stage of the journey the column of prisoners was well spread out, and some of the prisoners were obviously experiencing a variety of responses from the local inhabitants depending upon their relative position in the column as it straggled through the countryside to Lubeck. Individuals and groups were now engaged in virtually continuous bartering with the local farmers, often leaving and rejoining the column without interference from the guards. By 28 April the main part of the column had arrived at Wulmenau, just a few kilometres from Lubeck. Here once again the inhabitants were more than friendly, anxious to please and bartering resulted in the provision of reasonable meals including eggs. In some instances the outcome was an invitation to share a meal at a private home.

On 29 April the column renewed its leisurely pace, and that night everyone was awakened by a major artillery barrage, which turned out to be the crossing of the Elbe River by the advancing British armies. This immediately resulted in a variety of rumours, and coupled with the spectacle of retreating German soldiers throwing away their equipment and making friendly overtures, it was readily apparent the war was virtually at an end.

Dick Bartlett sadly recalls a tragic, almost unbelievable, incident that took place on or about 2 May. Apparently one of the POWs had walked quite normally into an adjacent field to scavenge some turnips to supplement the still inadequate rations. Upon his return, and to the utter dismay, shock and anger of his nearby fellow prisoners, a single, bloody minded trigger happy guard, for some inexplicable reason raised his rifle, shot and instantly killed the helpless POW. Those of the column that saw this unbelievable act, which took place with liberation and the war's end at hand, were not only helpless to prevent the murder but speechless with rage.

Shortly after a small British armoured scout car arrived and the incident was immediately reported to the officer. Recognizing that there still existed an unruly element among the guards, the car sped off only to be followed shortly after by the arrival of a British Sherman tank. The murderous guard was immediately identified and taken into custody. The battle weary British crew of the tank had gone through months of heavy fighting and witnessed shocking atrocities, which included releasing the 'walking dead' victims of the extermination camps. After hearing the details of the wanton murder of the POW by the guard they were in no mood to observe the niceties of war as it pertained to the deliberate murder of an innocent prisoner. They chose to exercise immediate 'vigilante justice'. Without any further delay the tank crew tied the guilty man to a tree, backed up the tank, aimed and fired a 75mm. round. The tree trunk and hapless German guard were instantly blown to pieces.

On the night of 4 May, Dick remembers that the German guards deserted the column, which by this time was quite widely dispersed, camping in various fields and in some cases wandering around searching to barter for food, or else heading for Lubeck which was now in British hands.

On the morning of 5 May a British army tank rumbled up to the field where several of the POWs were encamped. As Dick recounted, the British army Colonel in charge of the detachment, upon looking at the bearded, scruffy ragged prisoners, made the pessimistic comment that it would probably take two weeks to document the POWs, clear out the camp and return them all to the UK. This opinion was quickly discounted by many of the column. As Dick remembers, the area was quickly vacated by nightfall through the expeditious use of the British army transports, which were bringing up reinforcements to the area and returning empty. Dick was overwhelmed by the generous response of the transport drivers and remains forever grateful to them as they took all the POWs in the immediate area back to their reinforcement holding units. Here, deloused and showered, the prisoners were provided with fresh army uniforms and warmly welcomed by making available all the facilities of the unit. There was, however, an overriding concern among the newly released prisoners that they would be caught up locally in an extended procedure for documentation and checking of records before the group could proceed to England.

By 7 May, through direct intervention by some of the RAF POWs, arrangements were made for a number of the prisoners, of whom Dick was one, to be transported to an RAF airfield operating at Luneburg, where a squadron of Lancaster bombers was ferrying POWs back to England. So, after nearly five years as one of the first naval prisoners of war, Dick Bartlett finally achieved freedom and arrived back in familiar England.

By his estimate Dick calculated that the prisoners from the North Compound column of Stalag Luft 3 had struggled over 500 unbearable kilometres before finally achieving their liberation. They had experienced some of the most degrading and deadly suffering a human could endure. Weak, frozen and starving, their resolve to live eroded by the bitter cold, many fell by the wayside and for them it was a march of death. For the remainder, a sheer determination to live was the major factor in their struggle for survival. Although never prepared to face the appalling conditions which confronted them, they succeeded, overcoming a brutal, sometimes deadly, but always relentless period of unbelievable exposure to one of the coldest, bitter winters on record.

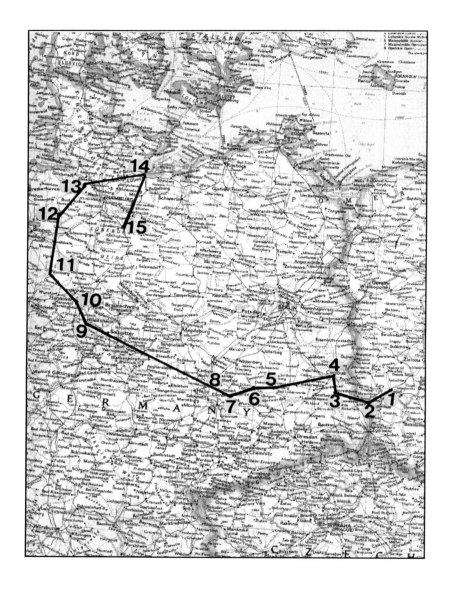

CHRONOLOGICAL LIST OF
DESTINATIONS DURING THE DESPERATE EXODUS

1	Stalag Luft 3, Sagan
2	Priebus
3	Spremburg
4	Cottbus
5	Falkenberg
6	Torgau
7	Eilenberg
8	Delitzsch
9	Hildesheim
10	Hanover
11	Nienburg
12	Tarnstedt (Marlag/Milag)
13	Blankenese
14	Lubeck
15	Luneberg

9

LIBERATED AND GOING HOME

U pon arrival in England the freed prisoners again went through delousing, had a medical and were issued new British army uniforms. Since four of this particular group were naval personnel, the RAF then sent a message to Portsmouth Naval Command to the effect that four naval POWs from Germany would be arriving at a specified time and transport was requested.

Much to the surprise, annoyance and discomfiture of the group, when they arrived at Portsmouth they were met by a naval prison 'paddy wagon' complete with armed Shore Patrol naval guards. Apparently the naval officer in charge at Portsmouth interpreted the message from the RAF concerning the four naval prisoners, to mean that they were German prisoners. LCdr. John Casson, Dick's original Commanding Officer, being one of the four, was so furious to be treated in such a churlish manner that he refused to be driven in a 'paddy wagon', particularly after spending five humbling years in German hands. He was finally convinced that if they did not use the vehicle further delay would no doubt take place in trying to resolve the problem. John Casson finally relented and did agree, so they were driven in 'fitting style' to the Naval Air Station at Lea-On-Solent, although it did take some time for him to eventually see the ironic humour of the incident.

There was one more hitch to Dick Bartletts 'welcome back'. As the only Canadian in the group, and after confirmation that he was indeed a POW in Germany, all his uniforms and kit had been sent back home to his father in Canada. So, unlike the others, he did not have immediate access to a proper naval officer's uniform. At Lee-On-Solent on the night of 8 May, VE Day, there was a large celebration in the officers wardroom. Since the remainder of his fellow prisoners had all departed and were joyfully reunited with their respective families, Dick was on his own. Not wanting to miss out on the action and be deprived of any such celebration, he decided to join the happy throng. Dressed only in a British Army privates uniform with no identifying rank or insignia, he was immediately singled out by the pompous Commander of the Mess and forthwith ordered out of the room for being improperly dressed. One understanding bar Steward, however, offered the loan of a white shirt, collar and tie, which Dick gratefully accepted and so he proceeded on his own to Portsmouth to have a drink and celebrate. But even this endeavour was abandoned as the enormous crowds jamming the streets and bars made any attempt on his part to have a drink impossible, so he ended up going to bed without having that longed for celebratory drink.

However, things brightened up the next day for Dick, as a new post-war life began with receipt of his back pay, new clothing and in no time at all he was back as a Royal Navy officer in a new uniform kit. The best news was yet to come, when he was informed that he was immediately entitled to three months leave. Great! thought Dick, as he had not seen his family for about eight years. Then the bad news! Royal Navy personnel were not allowed to take foreign leave during wartime. Not yet ready to give up he went to a friend, now a Commander at the Admiralty, and requested he be allowed to take a refresher flying course. Not so! All POWs were required to complete three months leave, then undergo a flying medical before any refresher course would be granted. The Commander did, however, pull some strings and quietly made arrangements for Dick to travel to Northern Ireland. Once there Dick, knowing that Canadian ships were frequently departing for Canada from Londonderry, believed with his travel experience of the past five years and his extensive 'on the job training' in escape and evasion, he should have no trouble going home to Canada and getting back into England.

As far as the Admiralty was concerned (if at all) Dick was now officially on leave in Northern Ireland. After arriving at Londonderry and making a few inquiries, Dick determined that a huge convoy was proceeding the next day for Canada and a genial corvette captain gave Dick the OK to hitch a ride, providing that he would stand a bridge watch from 0400-0600 each morning, and perhaps the occasional day watch as well. Dick was subsequently to have second thoughts about his selection of a corvette for his trans-Atlantic run.

He discovered very quickly that the ship bobbed up and down like a cork. Unused to three hearty meals a day, Dick also found out that his stomach was not used to such a motion. So, while on bridge duty at 0500, after the standard offer of a rich cup of cocoa from one of the watch-keeping sailors, the result was predictable. After a suitable waiting period for Dick to recover, the 'solicitous' sailor inquired whether the cocoa tasted better going down or coming back up!! It did not take long before Dick realized he was standing double duties, the first was watch keeping, the second providing entertainment for the sailors. The convoy pressed on and shortly after, one night somewhere off Newfoundland, the ships were advised that all the German submarines had now been accounted for and the convoy was now at liberty to disband. For the remainder of the night all the ships turned their lights on. As far as the eye could see the entire ocean was transformed into a great floating city, it was an unforgettable 'once in a lifetime' scene.

The next morning the convoy was well dispersed as the ships proceeded to their individual destinations. Dick's corvette went to St. Johns and he was told to await further instructions. So far things had gone well, but after visiting the Harbour Regulating Officer, to Dick's chagrin he was told that there was about a six week wait for passage to Halifax. However, his luck continued and after nosing around he located a frigate bound for Halifax, whose captain let him bunk in the officers wardroom for the two nights en route to Halifax.

Upon arrival Dick unthinkingly followed along with the crew of the frigate to exchange his British pounds for Canadian money to pay his train fare home. Unfortunately, an ever diligent paymaster Commander, upon spying Dick's Royal Navy identity card, was somewhat sceptical, knowing full well that Royal Navy officers were not allowed leave in foreign countries in wartime. Suspicious of Dick's status the Commander threatened to put him under close arrest. He did relent somewhat, but ordered him to consider himself under open arrest and report forthwith to the Stadacona wardroom while Dick's identity and situation were clarified.

Fortune again smiled upon Dick as he left, when the next sailor in the queue offered to exchange five pounds for equivalent Canadian money. These exchanges continued around the corner to the end of the line up of sailors and in no time he had accumulated $500 in Canadian funds and enough for the fare to Regina. He promptly went to the railway station and boarded the next train heading west. At this stage Dick had no qualms about disregarding the pay Commander's instruction, nor was he concerned about the regulation prohibiting war time leave visits to foreign countries.

After undergoing all his harrowing experiences over the past five years, Dick philosophically considered the current matter as rather trivial and nothing but a slight road bump on his journey back home. So, while those at the Admiralty had blithely assumed Dick was taking his recuperative leave quietly in North Ireland, he was happy and relaxed on a rapidly moving intercontinental train in a foreign country some 5000 miles distant, taking him back to his home which he had left some 7-8 years earlier. The trip home from this point on was uneventful and Dick thoroughly enjoyed the luxury of the train trip over the next few days, which was in marked contrast with his last ghastly train trip in a cattle car at the hands of the indifferent and often cruel German guards. Upon reaching Regina, Dick proceeded to Fort Qu'appelle, where he had a great family reunion for a month. However, this had to come to an end since, after expending one month in arriving, he calculated it would be better to allow the same amount of time to reach England.

On the eastward train back to Halifax Dick met some Australian servicemen, who were heading for Halifax to join an RN aircraft carrier returning to England. His good luck appeared to be holding, but unfortunately the train was three hours late in reaching Halifax. Much to his dismay he found the carrier had sailed and he and his Australian friends were now stranded.

Undaunted, Dick found out through discreet inquiries that a passenger ship was leaving shortly for England. Among those embarking was a group of 30 Canadian ex-RCAF pilots, who had recently transferred to the Royal Navy to join the rapidly expanding Fleet Air Arm and participate in the on-going war in the Pacific against Japan. The RN representative in charge of the group of Sub. Lt. pilots was an old Chief Petty Officer in a tiny office in the dockyard. He was delighted to assign Dick as First Lieutenant in charge of this group on the voyage across, which was gladly accepted in return for his passage.

It just so happened that among the passengers was a large contingent of Canadian army girls, which of course was a welcome addition to the passenger list. All was proceeding well as far as Dick was concerned until about the third day at sea, when an imposing female army Warrant officer with fire in her eyes accused Dick's young pilots of being involved in not so clandestine nightly visits to her female contingent, a practice which she ordered to cease forthwith. As Dick was to relate, after five years in Germany as a POW, facing this natural human instinct to seek out the opposite sex, he could only make a feeble effort to stop the visitations since his own inclination was to encourage such activities.

With his luck still holding, Dick arrived in London with a week to spare. Here he and one of his Australian friends found a room at the Strand Hotel for the princely sum of 15 shillings each, and for the next week, for the first time in over five years, he could celebrate with abandon and he became quickly acquainted with most of the night spots of London worth visiting. He then duly reported to the unsuspecting Admiralty, was processed, completed a medical and once more declared fit to fly.

By November 1945 Dick, now promoted to the rank of Lieutenant, and after completing a routine flying refresher on Harvard trainers, was thoroughly enjoying flying both Spitfire and Seafire operational fighter aircraft. These aircraft were lovely to fly and were indeed a far cry from the obsolete Skua in which Dick had flown his last fateful flight.

One day in late November he received a call to report to the Admiralty, only to be informed that his seven year commission with the Royal Navy was now completed. He was offered a permanent commission but Dick elected to turn down this offer and decided he preferred to return home to Canada. The Admiralty then informed him that the Canadian Navy was in the midst of forming its own Aviation Branch and was in the process of acquiring an aircraft carrier. The suggestion was then made that if Dick wanted to get a free ride home to Canada, joining the RCN was the way to go, since the Canadian carrier was due to depart the UK in March 1946. So, from the Admiralty he walked over to the RCN office and found to his pleasant surprise that his way home had already been cleared and he had been transferred from the Royal Navy over to the RCN.

In early 1946, Dick Bartlett joined 825 RCN Squadron which was now re-equipping with Firefly aircraft. The newly appointed squadron commander was no less than LCdr. O.W. 'Tats' Tattersall who had originally joined the Royal Navy with Dick Bartlett in 1938. 825 squadron and 803 fighter squadron were the first two Canadian naval squadrons to be formed and in March 1946 embarked the carrier HMCS *Warrior* and sailed for Halifax.

EPILOGUE

Following his transfer to the new Canadian Naval Aviation Branch and return to a full flying status, Dick elected to make a career in the RCN, and was transferred to the permanent force in January with the rank of Lieutenant. He continued to serve in 825 Firefly squadron as the Senior Pilot aboard the carrier HMCS *Warrior.* Sadly, on 31 January, 1947, the Commanding Officer LCdr. 'Tats' Tattersall was killed while flying near Victoria, B.C. This was a particularly tragic crash observing that Tattersall had flown throughout the war, had been awarded the Distinguished Service Cross, and was to end his life on a routine flight in peacetime.

Dick assumed command of the Firefly squadron, and in February 1947 was promoted to the acting rank of LCdr. In June he and Margaret Falconer were married and they both travelled overseas as the squadron was re-equipping with newer aircraft at RNAS Eglinton, Northern Ireland. Here the squadron worked up as the new aircraft carrier HMCS *Magnificent* was readied to replace *Warrior.*

Dick remained in his command while also enjoying the warm Irish hospitality until August 1948, when he was reappointed on the staff of the Director of Naval Aviation. In

May of 1950 he was confirmed in the rank of LCdr. and reappointed to another senior active flying position, assuming command of 18 Carrier Air Group, now re-equipped with a squadron of Avengers and a squadron of Sea Furies. He held this appointment for a year then subsequently assumed command of 30 Carrier Air Group until March 1952. Flying operations from HMCS *Magnificent* steadily increased in tempo and professionalism and Dick thoroughly enjoyed the opportunity to play a leading position in the rapidly expanding role the carrier and air groups played, as the ship and her escorts conducted major exercises in the Caribbean, Mediterranean and European waters.

Having achieved the position of air group commander, which in the fledgling new branch was the highest level of operational flying, Dick was now to expand his naval background since he was no longer eligible to continue in an active flying position. In his next appointment he was attached to the Staff of Flag Officer Atlantic Coast in the position of Staff Officer (Air), followed later in 1952 with appointments to sea aboard the cruiser HMCS *Quebec* and destroyers HMCS *Crescent* and HMCS *Sioux* to obtain his executive branch watch keeping certificate. On completion of this qualification Dick was then assigned to the RCAF Staff College Course in 1953. Following his Staff College graduation Dick was reappointed to Naval Headquarters in 1954 as Assistant Director of Naval Aviation.

In 1956 Dick was appointed back to the RCN Naval Air Station HMCS *Shearwater*. Here he completed an All Weather Flying Course and a Helicopter Familiarization Course. Then in 1957 he was reassigned to the much sought after appointment in the UK as Staff Office (Air) to the Naval

Member Canadian Joint Staff HMCS *Niobe* in London. Here he and his wife Margaret spent an enjoyable three years, with the opportunity of taking full advantage of all the amenities of the social life in London.

As Dick was to relate, all good things must come to an end and he was reappointed back to the bustling HMCS *Shearwater*, home of Canadian Naval Aviation, as LCdr. Flying, second in command of the station's air operations. By this time he was in a position to plan his final appointment, since he was due to retire within 18 months. His desire was to have his last tour of duty on the west coast, and since there was no aviation opportunities there he settled for a staff position as Assistant Secretary to the Flag Officer Pacific Coast, arriving at Victoria in 1962. He retired from the service in 1964 after a rewarding flying career in Canadian Naval Aviation.

Settled in Victoria, Dick and Margaret and their two children enjoyed life on the west coast and Dick, through his previous association with a tri-service investment fund which had since grown significantly, became instrumental in having it registered for sale in the province of Saskatchewan. However, this responsibility required a lot of travel and time away so Dick decided to retire once again.

Still with the flying bug alive Dick took on a short-lived job with Pacific Coastal Airways in the dual capacity of dispatcher and pilot. As Dick later related, he was not too impressed with some of their personnel and operating procedures so, by mutual agreement, he resigned from the airline.

In the Fall of 1964 Dick decided to return to his prairie roots and be his own boss, so he purchased a farm in

Saskatchewan. The first year everything went well, the crop was excellent and all appeared to be positive. He therefore decided to refinance his flourishing farming enterprise and expanded the operation by purchasing an adjacent farm, giving him a total of about 1,000 acres which in those days was a good viable farm. Unfortunately the next year the wheat market price collapsed, along with that of other grains.

To maintain his cash flow Dick went back to flying, taking a position with the province of British Columbia conducting aerial surveying and mapping. He found the government very co-operative and they soon worked out an arrangement which was satisfactory to both parties. Dick was given two weeks leave each Spring in order to find a retired farmer who would work for a reasonable wage, use Dick's farm equipment and run the farm. In the Fall he had another two weeks leave to return to the farm, sort out the finances and generally supervise the farm operations.

Dick thoroughly enjoyed the flying assignments which involved accurately mapping the northern third of British Columbia, a land mass of over 120,000 square miles or nearly the size of Germany. Since the area to be surveyed had to be clear of cloud, good weather was the norm.

There were, however, some significant challenges in the actual flying operations, since the aircraft he flew was a modified Beechcraft Expediter with limitations in the aircraft's equipment and high altitude performance. This was partially overcome by extending each wing by two feet which provided greater lift and gave a higher ceiling. Weight was reduced by removing surplus aircraft equipment and fixtures, consequently there was only one set of controls. The aircraft had a crew of three, comprising a pilot, camera operator and a maintenance technician. Ground radio aids were in many cases non-existent and airfields few and far between. The length of the sorties were anywhere from 4-6 hours, flying at a height of 20,000 feet. Oxygen facilities were definitely primitive, consisting of the pilot sucking on a hose connected to an oxygen cylinder.

Occasionally, when flying serenely along at altitude, the aircraft would hit subsiding pockets of air, which was not unusual in the mountainous areas. This in turn would often result in the aircraft losing as much as three to four thousand feet, and the camera picture footage would have to be repeated. Since the Beechcraft was flying at full throttle height, i.e. the throttles were wide open, a considerable amount of time was spent in regaining the lost altitude.

There were only two locations to base the aircraft, one was Watson Lake in the Yukon, the other was Prince George, B.C. and these were separated by a distance of 500 miles. Observing that they were flying over territory, most of which was acknowledged as being unmapped, any geographic references available were hardly reliable. Hence, navigation was by dead reckoning. Prior to the end of the day's mapping, and depending upon the miles covered, fuel state and estimated position, it was invariably necessary to make a choice as to which base was within aircraft range. As can be imagined in this type of flying the pilot's priority was fuel conservation, at which Dick became particularly adept as time went by.

He continued flying and maintaining the farm operation in this manner for two years, during which the Canadian agriculture sector improved considerably and the farm finances were back on track. He then assumed full time farming for another 10 years, living at the farm during the regular planting and cutting of the crops, and returning home to Victoria during the remainder of the year.

Dick finally decided to retire again and sold the farm in 1978, but at the request of an old friend did join with him in a partnership installing home insulation under a major retro fit program with federal funding support. Dick, however, had made a stipulation that he would only stay in the business for two years, and in 1980 he finally did retire for good.

Dick, now in his 85th year, with his wife Margaret are still enjoying a pleasant relaxing life, living in the outskirts of Victoria. Their genuine hospitality and caring manner is well known and greatly appreciated by their large circle of longtime friends. Dick is also an active member in the Victoria Chapter of the Canadian Naval Air Group. Each Fall he continues to make his special hunting trek to his home province of Saskatchewan, where he still manages to bag his annual limit of geese and duck. The Bartletts have a grown daughter Anne, a son James, and four grandsons.

In conclusion, it is noteworthy that Dick remains a longstanding and senior member of that very special group of veterans who comprise the POW Association. Each year he travels to their annual meeting in London, England. In September 2004 he once more made the trip. Sadly, but not unexpected, the number of attendees has dwindled steadily over the years and only about a dozen or so stalwarts mustered at the gathering. Joe Hill, Dick's longtime friend, was there. He was the only other one present who shared with Dick that fateful morning of 13 June, 1940, during a desperate time, requiring desperate measures, when a virtually hopeless air attack was carried out by a small group of courageous airmen.

Stuart Soward,
February 2005

55°30' N, 104°59' W,

Bartlett Lake

Named in Memory of

Christopher S. Bartlett

Son of Christopher Pennycuik Bartlett & Dora Margaret Bartlett

Fort Qu'Appelle, Saskatchewan

Royal Air Force - 39928
Wing Commander
D.F.C. & Bar

On Active Service To His Country
Killed in Action
June 13, 1944
Age 26
Buried at
Calais Canadian War Cemetery
France

This plaque of a previously unnamed lake in Saskatchewan was renamed Bartlett Lake by the Province of Saskatchewan following WW2. Such lakes were named for distinguished native sons killed during the war. In 1999, 15 members of the Bartlett family gathered on the lake shore and dedicated the plaque in honour of Wing Commander Christopher Bartlett, RAF, DFC and Bar.

Lt. Dick Bartlett in Seafire fighter.

Lt. Dick Bartlett, senior pilot of 825 Firefly squadron, 1946.

Lt. Commander Dick Bartlett.
Ottawa 1955

Dick Bartlett in the mid
1990s, Victoria.

SOURCES OF MATERIAL

A FORMIDABLE HERO - Stuart E. Soward 1987

THE CAMP - November 1987 issue and November 2003 issue

ESCAPE FROM THE SWASTIKA - Published by Marshall Cavendish 1953

FORCED MARCH TO FREEDOM - Robert Buckham 1984/1990

HANDS TO FLYING STATIONS VOL I - Stuart Soward 1993

THE LAST ESCAPE - John Nichol and Tony Rennell 2002

LIE IN THE DARK AND LISTEN - Wing Commander Ken Rees with Karen Arrandale 2004

LISTEN TO US - AIRCREW MEMORIES - Aircrew Association, Vancouver Island Branch 1997

THEY HAVE THEIR EXITS - Airey Neave 1953

INDEX

Lieutenant Commander Stuart E. Soward, CD, RCN (Rtd), served in the Royal Canadian Air Force, Royal Navy Volunteer Reserve (FAA) and the Royal Canadian Navy as a pilot for over 26 years. One of the first Canadian pilots to join the Canadian Naval Air Branch, he served as a member of 825 Squadron aboard Canada's first aircraft carrier HMCS *Warrior* in March 1946. He was an active aviator in several operational squadrons serving extensively aboard HMCS *Magnificent* and HMCS *Bonaventure* and ashore at the naval air station HMCS *Shearwater* at Dartmouth N.S.

In 1955 he was commended by the Chief of the Naval Staff for the invention of an improved aircraft night landing signals system. He assumed command of a naval air squadron in 1961, then was appointed to Naval Headquarters as a member of the Naval Aviation Directorate. He assumed additional duties at that time as the technical advisor on the research and preparation of the official history of Canadian Naval Aviation published in 1965. He retired in 1970, and over his service career flew over 15 military aircraft which included such operational naval carrier aircraft as the Firefly, Avenger, Hellcat, Bearcat, Sea Fury and Tracker.

In 1982 he was a contributor to the publication RCN in Retrospect, having presented a paper at that conference. In 1987 his first book, 'A Formidable Hero' was published. In 1992 he contributed an article on Maritime Command published in the Defence Associations National News Network. This was followed by his two volume recollective history of Canadian Naval Aviation, 'Hands To Flying Stations' Vols I and II, published in 1993 and 1995 respectively. He remains active in military and defence matters having made a submission to the Special Joint Committee on Canada's Defence Policy in 1994 and presented papers at the 1997 Conference Canada's Pacific Naval Presence and at the 4th Annual Air Force Historical Conference in 1998.

He is a past member of the Royal Navy Fleet Air Arm Officers Association, currently a member of the Canadian Naval Air Group and resides in Victoria, B.C. In 2005 he was awarded the Minister of Veterans Affairs Commendation.